XAMonline, Inc.
25 First Street, Suite 106
Cambridge, MA 02141
Toll Free: 1-800-509-4128
Email: info@xamonline.com
Web: www.xamonline.com
Fax: 1-617-583-5552

Library of Congress Cataloging-in-Publication Data

Wynne, Sharon A.
PLACE Elementary Education 01 Practice Test 1: Teacher Certification / Sharon A. Wynne. -1st ed.
ISBN: 978-1-60787-261-0
1. PLACE Elementary Education 01 Practice Test 1
2. Study Guides 3. PLACE 4. Teachers' Certification & Licensure
5. Careers

Disclaimer:
The opinions expressed in this publication are the sole works of XAMonline and were created independently from the National Education Association, Educational Testing Service, or any State Department of Education, National Evaluation Systems or other testing affiliates.

Between the time of publication and printing, state specific standards as well as testing formats and website information may change that is not included in part or in whole within this product. Sample test questions are developed by XAMonline and reflect similar content as on real tests; however, they are not former tests. XAMonline assembles content that aligns with state standards but makes no claims nor guarantees teacher candidates a passing score. Numerical scores are determined by testing companies such as NES or ETS and then are compared with individual state standards. A passing score varies from state to state.

Printed in the United States of America **œ-1**
PLACE Elementary Education 01 Practice Test 1
ISBN: 978-1-60787-261-0

Elementary Education
Pre-Test Sample Questions

READING

1. **To make a prediction a reader must:**
   (Average)

   A. Use text clues to evaluate the text at an inferential level

   B. Find a line of reasoning on which to rely

   C. Make a decision based on an observation

   D. Use prior knowledge and apply it to the current situation

2. **Which of the following is NOT a characteristic of a good reader?**
   (Rigorous)

   A. When faced with unfamiliar words, they skip over them unless meaning is lost

   B. They formulate questions that they predict will be answered in the text

   C. They establish a purpose before reading

   D. They go back to reread when something doesn't make sense

3. **All of the following are true about schemata EXCEPT:**
   (Rigorous)

   A. Used as a basis for literary response

   B. Structures that represent concepts stored in our memories

   C. A generalization that is proven with facts

   D. Used together with prior knowledge for effective reading comprehension.

4. **Children are taught phonological awareness when they are taught all but which concept?**
   (Average)

   A. The sounds made by the letters

   B. The correct spelling of words

   C. The sounds made by various combinations of letters

   D. The ability to recognize individual sounds in words

5. Which of the following is true about semantics?
(Average)

A. Semantics will sharpen the effect and meaning of a text

B. Semantics refers to the meaning expressed when words are arranged in a specific way.

C. Semantics is a vocabulary instruction technique.

D. Semantics is representing spoken language through the use of symbols.

6. Spelling instruction should include:
(Average)

A. Breaking down sentences

B. Developing a sense of correct and incorrect spellings

C. Identifying every word in a given text

D. Spelling words the way that they sound

7. Answering questions, monitoring comprehension, and interacting with a text are common methods of:
(Average)

A. Whole-class instruction

B. Comprehension instruction

C. Research-based instruction

D. Evidence-based instruction

8. Mrs. Young is a first grade teacher trying to select a books that are "just right" for her students to read independently. She needs to consider which of the following:
(Rigorous)

A. Illustrations should support the meaning of the text

B. Content that relates to student interest and experiences

C. Predictable text structures and language patterns

D. All of the above

9. **Which of the following is NOT characteristic of a folktale?**
(Average)

A. Considered true among various societies

B. A hero on a quest

C. Good versus evil

D. Adventures of animals

10. **Which of the following did NOT contribute to a separate literature genre for adolescents?**
(Rigorous)

A. The social changes of post–World War II

B. The Civil Rights movement

C. An interest in fantasy and science fiction

D. Issues surrounding teen pregnancy

11. **Which of the following is important in understanding fiction?**
(Rigorous)

I. Realizing the artistry in telling a story to convey a point.
II. Knowing fiction is imaginary.
III. Seeing what is truth and what is perspective.
IV. Acknowledging the difference between opinion and truth.

A. I and II only

B. II and IV only

C. III and IV only

D. IV only

12. **Assonance is a poetic device where:**
(Average)

A. The vowel sound in a word matches the same sound in a nearby word, but the surrounding consonant sounds are different

B. The initial sounds of a word, beginning either with a consonant or a vowel, are repeated in close succession

C. The words used evoke meaning by their sounds

D. The final consonant sounds are the same, but the vowels are different

13. Which of the following is true of the visible shape of poetry? ***(Rigorous)***

I. Forced sound repetition may underscore the meaning.
II. It was a new rule of poetry after poets began to feel constricted by rhyming conventions.
III. The shaped reflected the poem's theme.
IV. It was viewed as a demonstration of ingenuity.

A. I and II only

B. II and IV only

C. III and IV only

D. IV only

14. "Reading maketh a full man, conference a ready man, and writing an exact man" is an example of which type of figurative language? ***(Average)***

A. Euphemism

B. Bathos

C. Parallelism

D. Irony

15. Which of the following is NOT a strategy of teaching reading comprehension? **(*Rigorous)***

A. Summarization

B. Utilizing graphic organizers

C. Manipulating sounds

D. Having students generate questions

16. Which of the following sentences contains a subject-verb agreement error? ***(Average)***

A. Both mother and her two sisters were married in a triple ceremony

B. Neither the hen nor the rooster is likely to be served for dinner

C. My boss, as well as the company's two personnel directors, have been to Spain

D. Amanda and the twins are late again

17. **Which of the following are punctuated correctly?**
(Rigorous)

   I. **The teacher directed us to compare Faulkner's three symbolic novels *Absalom, Absalom*; *As I Lay Dying;* and *Light in August*.**
   II. **Three of Faulkner's symbolic novels are: *Absalom, Absalom*; *As I Lay Dying;* and *Light in August*.**
   III. **The teacher directed us to compare Faulkner's three symbolic novels: *Absalom, Absalom*; *As I Lay Dying;* and *Light in August*.**
   IV. **Three of Faulkner's symbolic novels are *Absalom, Absalom*; *As I Lay Dying;* and *Light in August*.**

A. I and II only

B. II and III only

C. III and IV only

D. IV only

18. **All of the following are true about verb tense EXCEPT:**
(Rigorous)

A. Present perfect tense is used to express action or a condition that started in the past and is continued to or completed in the present

B. Future tense is used to express a condition of future time

C. Past perfect tense expresses action or a condition that occurred as a precedent to some other action or condition

D. Future participial tense expresses action that started in the past or present and will conclude at some time in the future

19. **Which sentence is NOT correct?**
(Rigorous)

A. He ought not to get so angry.

B. I should of gone to bed.

C. I had set the table before dinner.

D. I have lain down.

20. All of the following are true about a descriptive essay EXCEPT:
(Average)

A. Its purpose is to make an experience available through one of the five senses

B. Its words make it possible for the reader to see with their mind's eye

C. Its language will move people because of the emotion involved

D. It is not trying to get anyone to take a certain action

21. A student has written a paper with the following characteristics: written in first person; characters, setting, and plot; some dialogue; events organized in chronological sequence with some flashbacks. In what genre has the student written?
(Rigorous)

A. Expository writing

B. Narrative writing

C. Persuasive writing

D. Descriptive writing

22. All of the following are stages of the writing process EXCEPT:
(Average)

A. Prewriting

B. Revising

C. Organizing

D. Presenting

23. Which of the following should not be included in the opening paragraph of an informative essay?
(Average)

A. Thesis sentence

B. Details and examples supporting the main idea

C. Broad general introduction to the topic

D. A style and tone that grabs the reader's attention

24. A sentence that contains one independent clause and three dependent clauses best describes a:
(Average)

A. Simple sentence

B. Compound sentence

C. Complex sentence

D. Compound-complex sentence

25. The main idea of a paragraph or story:
(Average)

A. Is what the paragraph or story is about.

B. Indicates what the passage is about.

C. Gives more information about the topic.

D. States the important ideas that the author wants the reader to know about a topic.

26. A strong topic sentence will:
(Rigorous)

A. Be phrased as a question

B. Always be the first sentence in a paragraph

C. Both A and B

D. Neither A nor B

27. Which of the following is a great way to keep a natural atmosphere when speaking publicly?
(Average)

A. Speak slowly

B. Maintain a straight, but not stiff, posture

C. Use friendly gestures

D. Take a step to the side every once in a while

28. Students returning from a field trip to the local newspaper want to thank their hosts for the guided tour. As their teacher, what form of communication should you encourage them to use?
(Rigorous)

A. Each student will send an e-mail expressing his or her appreciation

B. As a class, students will create a blog, and each student will write about what they learned

C. Each student will write a thank you letter that the teacher will fax to the newspaper

D. Each student will write a thank you note that the teacher will mail to the newspaper

29. Which of the following skills can help students improve their listening comprehension? *(Rigorous)*

I. Tap into prior knowledge.
II. Look for transitions between ideas.
III. Ask questions of the speaker.
IV. Discuss the topic being presented.

A. I and II only

B. II and IV only

C. II and IV only

D. IV only

30. As Ms. Wolmark looks at the mandated vocabulary curriculum for the 5th grade, she notes that she can opt to teach foreign words and abbreviations which have become part of the English language. She decides: *(Rigorous)*

A. To forego that since she is not a teacher of foreign language.

B. To teach only foreign words from the native language of her four ELL students.

C. To use the ELL students' native languages as a start for an extensive study of foreign language words.

D. To teach 2-3 foreign language words that are now in English and let it go at that.

MATH

1. **A truck rental company charges $40 per day plus $2.50 per mile. The odometer reading is *M* miles when a customer rents a truck and *m* miles when it is returned *d* days later. Which expression represents the total charge for the rental? *(Rigorous)***

   A. $40d + 2.5M - m$

   B. $40d + 2.5m - M$

   C. $40d + 2.5(M - m)$

   D. $40d + 2.5(m - M)$

2. **Using a pattern is an appropriate strategy for which of the following:**

   I Skip counting
   II Counting backward
   III Finding doubles

   (Easy)

   A. I and II

   B. I and III

   C. II and III

   D. I, II, and III

3. **The following set of numbers is not closed under addition: *(Rigorous)***

   A. Set of all real numbers

   B. Set of all even numbers

   C. Set of all odd numbers

   D. Set of all rational numbers

4. **What is the value of the following expression?**

$$\frac{25 - 2(6 - 2 \bullet 3)}{^{-}5(2 + 2 \bullet 4)}$$

   (Rigorous)

   A. 0.5

   B. 5.0

   C. -0.5

   D. 3.4

5. Which of the following expressions are equivalent to $28 - 4 \bullet 6 + 12$?

I $(28 - 4) \bullet 6 + 12$
II $28 - (4 \bullet 6) + 12$
III $(28 - 4) \bullet (6 + 12)$
IV $(28 + 12) - (4 \bullet 6)$
V $28 - 4 \bullet 12 + 6$

(Average)

A. I and V

B. II and IV

C. III and V

D. IV and V

6. If *n* represents an odd number, which of the following does not represent an even number?
(Average)

A. $2n$

B. $2(n + 1)$

C. n^2

D. $10n - 2$

7. Based upon the following examples, can you conclude that the sum of two prime numbers is also a prime number? Why or why not?

$$2 + 3 = 5$$
$$2 + 5 = 7$$
$$11 + 2 = 13$$

(Rigorous)

A. Yes, there is a pattern.

B. Yes, there are many more examples, such as 17 + 2 = 19 and 29 + 2 = 31.

C. No, there are many counterexamples

D. No, the sums are not prime numbers

8. If *x* is a whole number, what is the best description of the number $4x + 1$?
(Rigorous)

A. Prime number

B. Composite number

C. Odd number

D. Even number

9. The plot for a proposed new city hall plaza is 120 feet long by 90 feet wide. A scale model for the plaza must fit in an area that is 10 feet square. If the largest possible model is built in that area, what will be the maximum possible width for the scale model?
(Rigorous)

A. $\frac{2}{15}$ ft.

B. $1\frac{1}{3}$ ft.

C. $7\frac{1}{2}$ ft.

D. $13\frac{1}{3}$ ft.

10. Jocelyn wants create a magnetic board in the back of her classroom by covering part of the wall with a special magnetic paint. Each can of paint will cover 15 square feet. If the area is 12 feet wide and 8 feet high, how many cans of paint should she buy?
(Average)

A. 5 cans

B. 6 cans

C. 7 cans

D. 8 cans

11. A recipe makes 6 servings and calls for $1\frac{1}{2}$ cups of rice. How much rice is needed to make 10 servings?
(Average)

A. 2 cups

B. $2\frac{1}{4}$ cups

C. $2\frac{1}{2}$ cups

D. $2\frac{3}{4}$ cups

12. Which table(s) represents solutions of the following equation?

$$2x - 5y = 50$$

I

x	$^{-}5$	0	5	10
y	$^{-}12$	$^{-}10$	$^{-}8$	$^{-}6$

II

x	$^{-}5$	0	5	$^{-}10$
y	$^{-}12$	$^{-}10$	$^{-}12$	$^{-}10$

III

x	20	25	30	35
y	$^{-}2$	0	2	4

(Rigorous)

A. I

B. II

C. II and III

D. I and III

13. The relations given below demonstrate the following addition and multiplication property of real numbers:

a + b = b + a
ab = ba

(Average)

A. Commutative

B. Associative

C. Identity

D. Inverse

14. Which property (or properties) is applied below?

$$\begin{aligned} {}^{-}8x + 5x &= ({}^{-}8 + 5)x \\ &= {}^{-}3x \end{aligned}$$

I Associative Property of Addition
II Zero Property of Addition
III Additive Inverses
IV Identity Property of Multiplication
V Distributive Property

(Rigorous)

A. I

B. V

C. I and III

D. II and IV

15. For which of the following is the additive inverse equal to the multiplicative inverse? *(Rigorous)*

A. $\frac{2}{3}+\frac{3}{2}$

B. $\sqrt{-1}$

C. $\frac{1-\sqrt{2}}{1+\sqrt{2}}$

D. $(a+b)/(b-a)$

16. Which of the statements below explain the error(s), if any, in the following calculation?

$$\frac{18}{18} + 23 = 23$$

I A number divided by itself is 1, not 0.
II The sum of 1 and 23 is 24, not 23.
III The 18s are "cancelled" and replaced by 0.

(Rigorous)

A. I and II

B. II and III

C. I, II, and III

D. There is no error

17. **Which statement is a model for the following problem?**

27 less than 5 times a number is 193.

(Average)

A. $27 < 5x + 193$

B. $27 - 5x < 193$

C. $5x - 27 < 193$

D. $5x - 27 = 193$

18. **What is the solution set of the following inequality?**

$$4x + 9 \geq 11(x - 3)$$

(Average)

A. $x \leq 0$

B. $x \geq 0$

C. $x \leq 6$

D. $x \geq 6$

19. **A car is rented in Quebec. The outside temperature shown on the dashboard reads 17°C. What is the temperature in degrees Fahrenheit? (Use the formula $F = \frac{9}{5}C + 32$.)**

(Average)

A. 27.2°*F*

B. 41.4°*F*

C. 62.6°*F*

D. 88.2°*F*

20. **The two solutions of the quadratic equation $ax^2 + bx + c = 0$ are given by the formula**

$$x = \frac{-b \pm \sqrt{b^2 - 4ac}}{2a}.$$

What are the solutions of the equation $x^2 - 18x + 32$?
(Rigorous)

A. ⁻5 and 23

B. 2 and 16

C. $9 \pm \sqrt{113}$

D. $9 \pm 2\sqrt{113}$

21. Triangle *ABC* is rotated 90° clockwise about the origin and translated 6 units left.

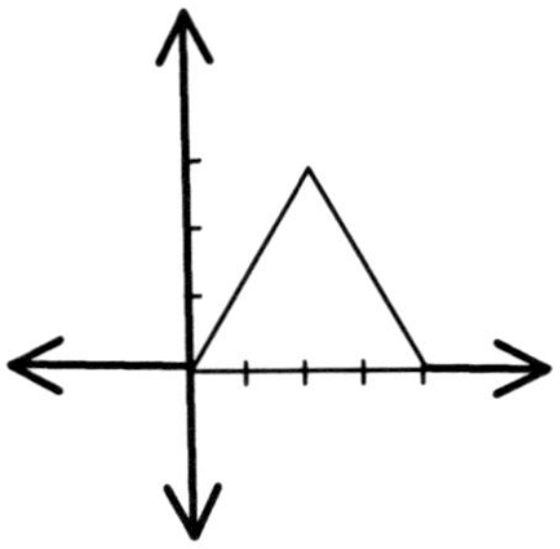

What are the coordinates of *B* after the transformations?
(Rigorous)

A. $(2, {}^{-}3)$

B. $(3, {}^{-}2)$

C. $({}^{-}2, {}^{-}3)$

D. $({}^{-}3, {}^{-}2)$

22. The following represents the net of a

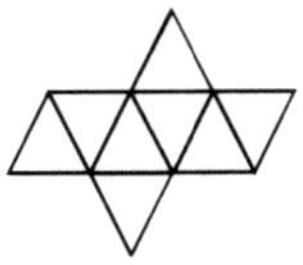

(Average)

A. Cube

B. Tetrahedron

C. Octahedron

D. Dodecahedron

23. Ginny and Nick head back to their respective colleges after being home for the weekend. They leave their house at the same time and drive for 4 hours. Ginny drives due south at the average rate of 60 miles per hour and Nick drives due east at the average rate of 0 miles per hour. What is the straight-line distance between them, in miles, at the end of the 4 hours?
(Rigorous)

A. 169.7 miles

B. 240 miles

C. 288 miles

D. 339.4 miles

24. What is the surface area of the prism shown below?
(Rigorous)

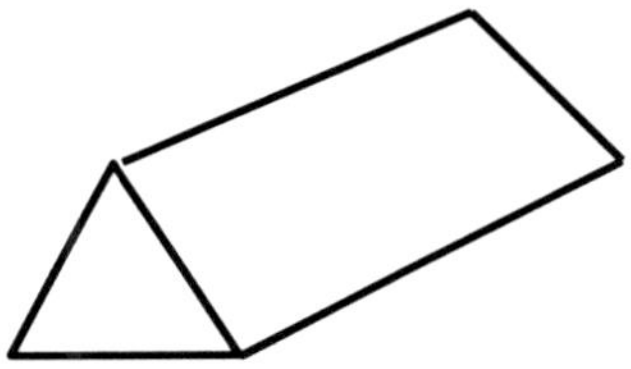

A. 204 cm^2

B. 216 cm^2

C. 360 cm^2

D. 180 cm^2

25. Which of the following is not equivalent to 3 km?

I 3.0×10^3 m
II 3.0×10^4 cm
III 3.0×10^6 mm

(Average)

A. I

B. II

C. III

D. None of the above

26. A school band has 200 members. Looking at the pie chart below, determine which statement is true about the band.
(Average)

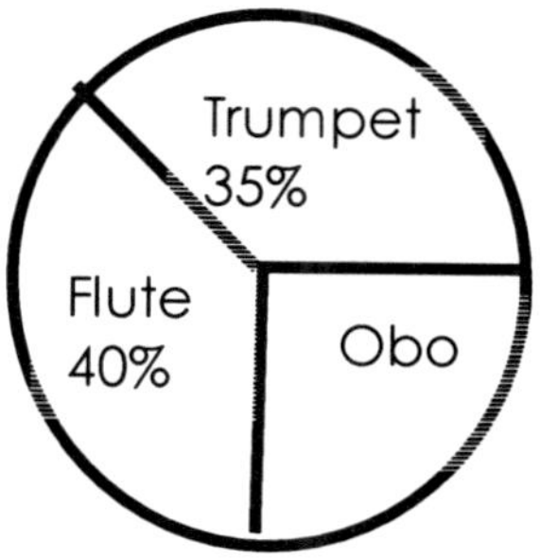

A. There are more trumpet players than flute players

B. There are fifty oboe players in the band

C. There are forty flute players in the band

D. One-third of all band members play the trumpet

27. A restaurant offers the following menu choices.

Green Vegetable	Yellow Vegetable
Asparagus	Carrots
Broccoli	Corn
Peas	Squash
Spinach	

If a customer chooses a green vegetable and a yellow vegetable at random, what is the probability that the customer will order neither asparagus nor corn?
(Rigorous)

A. $\frac{1}{12}$

B. $\frac{1}{6}$

C. $\frac{1}{3}$

D. $\frac{1}{2}$

28. A school has 15 male teachers and 35 female teachers. In how many ways can they form a committee with 2 male teachers and 4 female teachers on it?
(Average)

A. 525

B. 5497800

C. 88

D. 263894400

29. A music store owner wants to change the window display every week. Only 4 out of 6 instruments can be displayed in the window at the same time. How many weeks will it be before the owner must repeat the same arrangement (in the same order) of instruments in the window display?
(Rigorous)

A. 24 weeks

B. 36 weeks

C. 120 weeks

D. 360 weeks

30. Half the students in a class scored 80% on an exam; one student scored 10%; and the rest of the class scored 85%. Which would be the best measure of central tendency for the test scores?
(Rigorous)

A. Mean

B. Median

C. Mode

D. Either the median or the mode because they are equal

SOCIAL SCIENCES

1. **The Great Plains in the United States are an excellent place to grow corn and wheat for all of the following reasons EXCEPT:** ***(Average)***

   A. Rainfall is abundant and the soil is rich

   B. The land is mostly flat and easy to cultivate

   C. The human population is modest in size, so there is plenty of space for large farms

   D. The climate is semitropical

2. **What is characteristic of areas of the world with high populations?** ***(Rigorous)***

   A. These areas tend to have heavy pollution

   B. These areas are almost always surrounded by suburbs

   C. Populations are rarely located near one another

   D. Most populated places in the world also tend to be close to agricultural lands

3. **Meridians, or lines of longitude, not only help in pinpointing locations but are also used for:** ***(Average)***

   A. Measuring distance from the Poles

   B. Determining direction of ocean currents

   C. Determining the time around the world

   D. Measuring distance on the equator

4. **The Western Hemisphere contains all of which of the following continents?** ***(Rigorous)***

   A. Russia

   B. Europe

   C. North America

   D. Asia

5. Mr. Allen is discussing the earthquake in Chile and explains the aftershocks and tsunamis that threatened Pacific islands thousands of miles away. What aspect of geographical studies was he emphasizing?
(Rigorous)

A. Regional

B. Topical

C. Physical

D. Human

6. Which of the following are non-renewable resources?
(Average)

A. Fish, coffee, and forests

B. Fruit, water, and solar energy

C. Wind power, alcohol, and sugar

D. Coal, natural gas, and oil

7. What people perfected the preservation of dead bodies?
(Average)

A. Sumerians

B. Phoenicians

C. Egyptians

D. Assyrians

8. Which of these is NOT a true statement about the Roman civilization?
(Rigorous)

A. Its period of Pax Romana provided long periods of peace during which travel and trade increased, enabling the spread of culture, goods, and ideas over the known world

B. It borrowed the concept of democracy from the Greeks and developed it into a complex representative government

C. It flourished in the arts with a realistic approach to art and a dramatic use of architecture

D. It developed agricultural innovations such as crop rotation and terrace farming

9. The major force in eighteenth and nineteenth century politics was:
(Average)

A. Nationalism

B. Revolution

C. War

D. Diplomacy

10. **The identification of individuals or groups as they are influenced by their own group or culture is called:** ***(Average)***

A. Cross-cultural exchanges

B. Cultural diffusion

C. Cultural identity

D. Cosmopolitanism

11. **The New England colonies included:** ***(Average)***

A. South Carolina

B. Georgia

C. Massachusetts

D. New York

12. **Which major economic activity of the Southern colonies led to the growth of slavery?** ***(Rigorous)***

A. Manufacturing

B. Fishing

C. Farming

D. Coal mining

13. **Which was the first instance of an internal tax on the American colonies?** ***(Average)***

A. The Proclamation Act

B. The Sugar Act

C. The Currency Act

D. The Stamp Act

14. **The Lewis and Clark expedition advanced knowledge in each of the following areas EXCEPT:** ***(Average)***

A. Geography

B. Modern warfare

C. Botany

D. Animal life

15. **Populism arises out of a feeling:** ***(Average)***

A. Of intense happiness

B. Of satisfaction with the activities of large corporations

C. That women should not be allowed to vote

D. Perceived oppression

16. **At the end of the Twentieth Century, the United States was:**
(Average)

A. A central leader in international affairs

B. A reluctant participant in international affairs

C. One of two superpowers

D. Lacking a large consumer culture

17. **How did manufacturing change in the early 1800s?**
(Rigorous)

A. The electronics industry was born

B. Production moved from small shops or homes into factories

C. Industry benefited from the Federal Reserve Act

D. The timber industry was hurt when Theodore Roosevelt set aside 238 million acres of federal lands to be protected from development

18. **The early ancient civilizations developed systems of government:**
(Rigorous)

A. To provide for defense against attack

B. To regulate trade

C. To regulate and direct the economic activities of the people as they worked together in groups

D. To decide on the boundaries of the different fields during planting seasons

19. **What is another name for dictatorship?**
(Rigorous)

A. Oligarchy

B. Monarchy

C. Anarchism

D. Communism

20. Which of the following documents described and defined the system and structure of the United States government?
(Average)

A. The Bill of Rights

B. The Declaration of Independence

C. The Constitution

D. The Articles of Confederation

21. How did the ideology of John Locke influence Thomas Jefferson in writing the Declaration of Independence?
(Rigorous)

A. Locke emphasized human rights and believed that people should rebel against governments who violated those rights

B. Locke emphasized the rights of government to protect its people and to levy taxes

C. Locke believed in the British system of monarchy and the rights of Parliament to make laws

D. Locke advocated individual rights over the collective whole

22. Which of the following is not a right declared by the U.S. Constitution?
(Average)

A. The right to speak out in public

B. The right to use cruel and unusual punishment

C. The right to a speedy trial

D. The right not to be forced to testify against yourself

23. The cold weather froze orange crops in Florida and the price of orange juice increased. This is an example of what economic concept?
(Rigorous)

A. Output market

B. Input market

C. Supply and demand

D. Entrepreneurship

24. What type of production process must producers choose?
(Average)

A. One that is inefficient

B. One that often produces goods that consumers don't want

C. One that is efficient

D. One that is sometimes efficient and sometimes inefficient

25. The existence of economics is based on:
(Rigorous)

A. The scarcity of resources

B. The abundance of resources

C. Little or nothing that is related to resources

D. Entrepreneurship

26. In the fictional country of Nacirema, the government controls the means of production and directs resources. It alone decides what will be produced; as a result, there is an abundance of capital and military goods but a scarcity of consumer goods. What type of economy is this?
(Rigorous)

A. Market economy

B. Centrally planned economy

C. Market socialism

D. Capitalism

27. Which of the following are secondary research materials?
(Average)

A. The conclusions and inferences of other historians

B. Literature and nonverbal materials, novels, stories, poetry, and essays from the period, as well as coins, archaeological artifacts, and art produced during the period

C. Interviews and surveys conducted by the researcher

D. Statistics gathered as the result of the research's experiments

28. For their research paper on the effects of the Civil War on American literature, students have brainstormed a list of potential online sources and are seeking your authorization. Which of these represent the strongest source?
(Rigorous)

A. http://www.wikipedia.org/

B. http://www.google.com

C. http://www.nytimes.com

D. http://docsouth.unc.edu /southlit/civilwar.html

29. For the historian studying ancient Egypt, which of the following would be least useful?
(Rigorous)

A. The record of an ancient Greek historian on Greek-Egyptian interaction

B. Letters from an Egyptian ruler to his/her regional governors

C. Inscriptions on stele of the Fourteenth Egyptian Dynasty

D. Letters from a nineteenth century Egyptologist to his wife

30. Which of the following can be considered the primary goal of social studies?
(Rigorous)

A. Recalling specific dates and places

B. Identifying and analyzing social links

C. Using contextual clues to identify eras

D. Linking experiments with history

SCIENCE

1. Which is the correct order for the layers of Earth's atmosphere?
(Easy)

A. Troposphere, stratosphere, mesosphere, and thermosphere

B. Mesosphere, stratosphere, troposphere, and thermosphere

C. Troposphere, stratosphere, thermosphere, and mesosphere

D. Thermosphere, troposphere, stratosphere, mesosphere

2. Which statement correctly describes the theory of plate tectonics?
(Easy)

A. There eight major plates and many small plates that move at a rate of 10 to 50 millimeters per year

B. There is one plate for each continent and they move at a speed too small to measure

C. There are thousands of plates that move 1 to 5 meters per year

D. Earthquakes are caused by the collision of plates

3. What type of rock can be classified by the size of the crystals in the rock?
(Easy)

A. Metamorphic

B. Igneous

C. Minerals

D. Sedimentary

4. What are solids with a definite chemical composition and a tendency to split along planes of weakness?
(Easy)

A. Ores

B. Rocks

C. Minerals

D. Salts

5. In which of the following eras did life appear?
(Easy)

A. Paleozoic

B. Mesozoic

C. Cenozoic

D. Precambrian

6. **The use of radioactivity to determine the age of rocks and fossils is called which of the following?**
(Easy)

A. Carbon dating

B. Absolute dating

C. Stratigraphy

D. Geological dating

7. **Which of the following astronomical entities is not part of the galaxy the Sun is located in?**
(Easy)

A. Nebulae

B. Quasars

C. Pulsars

D. Neutron stars

8. **Why is the winter in the southern hemisphere colder than winter in the northern hemisphere?**
(Average)

A. Earth's axis of 24-hour rotation tilts at an angle of 23□°

B. The elliptical orbit of Earth around the Sun changes the distance of the Sun from Earth

C. The southern hemisphere has more water than the northern hemisphere

D. The green house effect is greater for the northern hemisphere

9. **Which of the following facts of physics best explains the cause of tides?**
(Rigorous)

A. The density of water is less than the density of rock

B. The force of gravity follows the inverse square law

C. Centripetal acceleration causes water on Earth to bulge

D. The gravitational force of the Moon on Earth's oceans

10. Which of the following is not a property that eukaryotes have and prokaryotes do not have?
(Average)

A. Nucleus

B. Ribosomes

C. Chromosomes

D. Mitochondria

11. Which of the following processes and packages macromolecules?
(Easy)

A. Lysosomes

B. Cytosol

C. Golgi apparatus

D. Plastids

12. Which is not a characteristic of living organisms?
(Easy)

A. Sexual reproduction

B. Ingestion

C. Synthesis

D. Respiration

13. At what stage in mitosis does the chromatin become chromosomes?
(Average)

A. Telophase

B. Anaphase

C. Prophase

D. Metaphase

14. Meiosis starts with a single cell and ends with which of the following?
(Average)

A. Two diploid cells.

B. Two haploid cells.

C. Four diploid cells

D. Four haploid cells

15. How many autosomes are in somatic cells of human beings?
(Easy)

A. 22

B. 23

C. 44

D. 46

16. **Which of the following is not part of Darwinian evolution?** ***(Average)***

    A. Survival of the fittest

    B. Random mutations

    C. Heritability of acquired traits

    D. Natural selection

17. **Taxonomy classifies species into genera (plural of genus) based on similarities. Species are subordinate to genera. The most general or highest taxonomical group is the kingdom. Which of the following is the correct order of the other groups from highest to lowest?** ***(Easy)***

    A. Class ⇒ order⇒ family ⇒ phylum

    B. Phylum ⇒ class ⇒ family ⇒ order

    C. Phylum ⇒ class ⇒ order ⇒ family

    D. Order ⇒ phylum ⇒ class ⇒ family

18. **Which of the following describes the interaction between community members when one species feeds of another species but does not kill it immediately?** ***(Easy)***

    A. Parasitism

    B. Predation

    C. Commensalism

    D. Mutualism

19. **Which of the following statements about the density of a substance is true?** ***(Easy)***

    A. It is a chemical property

    B. It is a physical property

    C. It does not depend on the temperature of the substance

    D. It is a property only of liquids and solids

20. The electrons in a neutral atom that is not in an excited energy state are in various energy shells. For example, there are two electrons in the lowest energy shell and eight in the next shell if the atom contains more than 10 electrons. How many electrons are in the shell with the maximum number of electrons?
(Easy)

A. 8

B. 18

C. 32

D. 44

21. Which statement best explains why a balance scale is used to measure both weight and mass?
(Rigorous)

A. The weight and mass of an object are identical concepts

B. The force of gravity between two objects depends on the mass of the two objects

C. Inertial mass and gravitational mass are identical

D. A balance scale compares the weight of two objects

22. Which of the following does not determine the frictional force between a box sliding down a ramp?
(Average)

A. The weight of the box

B. The area of the box

C. The angle the ramp makes with the horizontal

D. The chemical properties of the two surfaces.

23. Which statement is true about temperature?
(Easy)

A. Temperature is a measurement of heat

B. Temperature is how hot or cold an object is

C. The coldest temperature ever measured is zero degrees Kelvin

D. The temperature of a molecule is its kinetic energy

24. When glass is heated, it becomes softer and softer until it becomes a liquid. Which of the following statements best describes this phenomenon?
(Rigorous)

A. Glass has no heat of vaporization

B. Glass has no heat of fusion

C. The latent heat of glass is zero calories per gram

D. Glass is made up of crystals

25. Which statement could be described as the first law of thermodynamics?
(Average)

A. No machine can convert heat energy to work with 100 percent efficiency

B. Energy is neither created nor destroyed

C. Thermometers can be used to measure temperatures

D. Heat flows from hot objects to cold objects

26. What kind of chemical reaction is the burning of coal?
(Average)

A. Exothermic and composition

B. Exothermic and decomposition

C. Endothermic and composition

D. Exothermic and decomposition

27. Which of the following is a result of a nuclear reaction called fission?
(Easy)

A. Sunlight

B. Cosmic radiation

C. Supernova

D. Existence of the elements in the periodic table

28. What is technology?
(Easy)

A. The application of science to satisfy human needs

B. Knowledge of complex machines, computer systems, and manufacturing processes

C. The study of engineering

D. A branch of science

29. **An experiment is performed to determine how the surface area of a liquid affects how long it takes for the liquid to evaporate. One hundred milliliters of water is put in containers with surface areas of 10 cm^2, 30 cm^2, 50 cm^2, 70 cm^2, and 90 cm^2. The time it took for each container to evaporate is recorded. Which of the following is a controlled variable?**
(Average)

A. The time required for each evaporation

B. The area of the surfaces

C. The amount of water

D. The temperature of the water

30. **Stars near Earth can be seen to move relative to fixed stars. In observing the motion of a nearby star over a period of decades, an astronomer notices that the path is not a straight line but wobbles about a straight line. The astronomer reports in a peer-reviewed journal that a planet is rotating around the star, causing it to wobble. Which of the following statements best describes the proposition that the star has a planet?**
(Rigorous)

A. Observation

B. Hypothesis

C. Theory

D. Inference

Elementary Education
Pre-Test Sample Questions with Rationales

READING

1. **To make a prediction a reader must:**
   (Average)

   A. Use text clues to evaluate the text at an inferential level

   B. Find a line of reasoning on which to rely

   C. Make a decision based on an observation

   D. Use prior knowledge and apply it to the current situation

Answer: A. Use text clues to evaluate the text at an inferential level.
Making a prediction requires the reader to evaluate a text by going beyond the literal level of what is stated to an inferential level by using text clues to make predictions as to what will happen next in the text. Because choices B–D do not involve evaluating a text on an inferential level, they are not correct ways to make a prediction.

2. **Which of the following is NOT a characteristic of a good reader?**
   (Rigorous)

   A. When faced with unfamiliar words, they skip over them unless meaning is lost

   B. They formulate questions that they predict will be answered in the text

   C. They establish a purpose before reading

   D. They go back to reread when something doesn't make sense

Answer: A. When faced with unfamiliar words, they skip over them unless meaning is lost
While skipping over an unknown word may not compromise the meaning of the text, a good reader will attempt to pronounce the word by using analogies to familiar words. They also formulate questions, establish a purpose, and go back to reread if meaning is lost.

3. All of the following are true about schemata EXCEPT:
(Rigorous)

A. Used as a basis for literary response

B. Structures that represent concepts stored in our memories

C. A generalization that is proven with facts

D. Used together with prior knowledge for effective reading comprehension

Answer: C. A generalization that is proven with facts
Schemata are structures that represent concepts stored in the memory. When used together with prior knowledge and ideas from the printed text while reading, comprehension takes place. Schemata have nothing to do with making a generalization and proving it with facts.

4. Children are taught phonological awareness when they are taught all but which concept?
(Average)

A. The sounds made by the letters

B. The correct spelling of words

C. The sounds made by various combinations of letters

D. The ability to recognize individual sounds in words

Answer: B. The correct spelling of words.
Phonological awareness happens during the pre-K years or even earlier and involves connecting letters to sounds. Children begin to develop a sense of correct and incorrect spellings of words in a transitional spelling phase that is traditionally entered in elementary school.

5. **Which of the following is true about semantics?**
(Average)

A. Semantics will sharpen the effect and meaning of a text

B. Semantics refers to the meaning expressed when words are arranged in a specific way

C. Semantics is a vocabulary instruction technique

D. Semantics is representing spoken language through the use of symbols

Answer: B. Semantics refers to the meaning expressed when words are arranged in a specific way
Understanding semantics means understanding that meaning is imbedded in the order of words in a sentence. Changing the order of the words would change the meaning of a sentence. The other three choices do not involve finding meaning through the order of words.

6. **Spelling instruction should include:**
(Average)

A. Breaking down sentences

B. Developing a sense of correct and incorrect spellings

C. Identifying every word in a given text

D. Spelling words the way that they sound

Answer: B. Developing a sense of correct and incorrect spellings
Developing a sense of correct and incorrect spellings is part of the developmental stages of spelling and is a phase that is typically entered later in elementary school. Breaking down sentences involves paragraph analysis, identifying every word in a given text is not necessary to construct meaning from that text, and spelling words the way that they sound is not an effective way to teach spelling.

7. **Answering questions, monitoring comprehension, and interacting with a text are common methods of:**
(Average)

A. Whole-class instruction

B. Comprehension instruction

C. Research-based instruction

D. Evidence-based instruction

Answer: B. Comprehension instruction
Comprehension instruction helps students learn strategies that they can use independently with any text. Answering questions, monitoring comprehension, and interacting with a text are a few strategies that teachers can teach to their students to help increase their comprehension. Research-based, evidence-based, and whole-class instruction relate to specific reading programs available.

8. **Mrs. Young is a first grade teacher trying to select a books that are "just right" for her students to read independently. She needs to consider which of the following:**
(Rigorous)

A. Illustrations should support the meaning of the text.

B. Content that relates to student interest and experiences

C. Predictable text structures and language patterns

D. All of the above

Answer: D. All of the above
It is important that all of the above factors be considered when selecting books for young children.

9. **Which of the following is NOT characteristic of a folktale?**
(Average)

A. Considered true among various societies

B. A hero on a quest

C. Good versus evil

D. Adventures of animals

Answer: A. Considered true among various societies
There are few societies that would consider folktales to be true as folktale is another name for fairy tale, and elements such as heroes on a quest, good versus evil, and adventures of animals are popular, fictional, themes in fairy tales.

10. **Which of the following did NOT contribute to a separate literature genre for adolescents?**
(Rigorous)

A. The social changes of post–World War II

B. The Civil Rights movement

C. An interest in fantasy and science fiction

D. Issues surrounding teen pregnancy

Answer: C. An interest in fantasy and science fiction
Social changes after World War II, the Civil Rights movement, and personal issues like teen pregnancy all contributed to authors writing a new breed of contemporary fiction to help adolescents understand and cope with the world they live in. Adolescents may be interested in fantasy and science fiction topics but that interest did not cause the creation of an entire genre.

11. Which of the following is important in understanding fiction?
(Rigorous)

I. Realizing the artistry in telling a story to convey a point.
II. Knowing fiction is imaginary.
III. Seeing what is truth and what is perspective.
IV. Acknowledging the difference between opinion and truth.

A. I and II only

B. II and IV only

C. III and IV only

D. IV only

Answer: A. I and II only
In order to understand a piece of fiction, it is important that readers realize that an author's choice in a work of fiction is for the sole purpose of conveying a viewpoint. It is also important to understand that fiction is imaginary. Seeing what is truth and what is perspective and acknowledging the difference between opinion and truth are important in understanding nonfiction.

12. **Assonance is a poetic device where:**
(Average)

A. The vowel sound in a word matches the same sound in a nearby word, but the surrounding consonant sounds are different

B. The initial sounds of a word, beginning either with a consonant or a vowel, are repeated in close succession

C. The words used evoke meaning by their sounds

D. The final consonant sounds are the same, but the vowels are different

Answer: A. The vowel sound in a word matches the same sound in a nearby word, but the surrounding consonant sounds are different
Assonance takes the middle territory of rhyming so that the vowel sounds are similar, but the consonant sounds are different: “tune” and “food” are assonant. Repeating words in close succession that have the same initial sound (“puppies who pant pathetically”) is alliteration. Using the sounds of words to evoke meaning (“zip, pow, pop”) is onomatopoeia. When final consonant sounds are the same and the vowels are different, and author has used a different kind of alliteration.

13. Which of the following is true of the visible shape of poetry?
(Rigorous)

I. Forced sound repetition may underscore the meaning.
II. It was a new rule of poetry after poets began to feel constricted by rhyming conventions.
III. The shaped reflected the poem's theme.
IV. It was viewed as a demonstration of ingenuity.

A. I and II only

B. II and IV only

C. III and IV only

D. IV only

Answer: C. III and IV only
During the seventeenth century, some poets shaped their poems on the page. The shape would reflect the poem's theme. While an interesting device, the skill was viewed as a demonstration of ingenuity but did not add to the effect or meaning of the poem. Sound repetition has no effect on the visible shape of a poem. Shaping a poem was never a rule all poets deemed to follow.

14. "Reading maketh a full man, conference a ready man, and writing an exact man" is an example of which type of figurative language?
(Average)

A. Euphemism

B. Bathos

C. Parallelism

D. Irony

Answer: C. Parallelism
Parallelism is the arrangement of ideas into phrases, sentences, and paragraphs that balance one element with another of equal importance and similar wording. In the example given, reading, conference, and writing are balanced in importance and wording. A euphemism substitutes an agreeable term for one that might offend. Bathos is a ludicrous attempt to evoke pity, sympathy, or sorrow. Irony is using an expression that is the opposite to the literal meaning.

15. Which of the following is NOT a strategy of teaching reading comprehension?
(Rigorous)

A. Summarization

B. Utilizing graphic organizers

C. Manipulating sounds

D. Having students generate questions

Answer: C. Manipulating sounds
Comprehension simply means that the reader can ascribe meaning to text. Teachers can use many strategies to teach comprehension, including questioning, asking students to paraphrase or summarize, utilizing graphic organizers, and focusing on mental images.

16. Which of the following sentences contains a subject-verb agreement error?
(Average)

A. Both mother and her two sisters were married in a triple ceremony

B. Neither the hen nor the rooster is likely to be served for dinner

C. My boss, as well as the company's two personnel directors, have been to Spain

D. Amanda and the twins are late again

Answer: C. My boss, as well as the company's two personnel directors, have been to Spain
In choice C, the true subject of the verb is "My boss," not "two personnel directors." Because the subject is singular, the verb form must be singular, "has." In choices A and D, the compound subjects are joined by "and" and take the plural form of the verb. In choice B, the compound subject is joined by "nor" so the verb must agree with the subject closer to the verb. "Rooster" is singular so the correct verb is "is."

17. Which of the following are punctuated correctly?
(Rigorous)

I. The teacher directed us to compare Faulkner's three symbolic novels *Absalom, Absalom*; *As I Lay Dying;* and *Light in August*.
II. Three of Faulkner's symbolic novels are: *Absalom, Absalom*; *As I Lay Dying;* and *Light in August*.
III. The teacher directed us to compare Faulkner's three symbolic novels: *Absalom, Absalom*; *As I Lay Dying;* and *Light in August*.
IV. Three of Faulkner's symbolic novels are *Absalom, Absalom*; *As I Lay Dying;* and *Light in August*.

A. I and II only

B. II and III only

C. III and IV only

D. IV only

Answer: C. III and IV only
These sentences are focusing on the use of a colon. The rule is to place a colon at the beginning of a list of items except when the list is preceded by a verb. Sentences I and III do not have a verb before the list and therefore need a colon. Sentences II and IV have a verb before the list and therefore do not need a colon.

18. All of the following are true about verb tense EXCEPT:
(Rigorous)

A. Present perfect tense is used to express action or a condition that started in the past and is continued to or completed in the present

B. Future tense is used to express a condition of future time

C. Past perfect tense expresses action or a condition that occurred as a precedent to some other action or condition

D. Future participial tense expresses action that started in the past or present and will conclude at some time in the future

Answer: D. Future participial tense expresses action that started in the past or present and will conclude at some time in the future
Choices A–C are correct statements about each type of verb tense. D is incorrect because there is no such thing as future participial tense.

19. Which sentence is NOT correct?
(Rigorous)

A. He ought not to get so angry.

B. I should of gone to bed.

C. I had set the table before dinner.

D. I have lain down.

Answer: B. I should of gone to bed.
The most frequent problems in verb use come from the improper formation of the past and past participial forms. Choices A, C, and D may sound awkward but are actually correct uses of the participial tense. "I should of gone to bed" is incorrect because "of" is not a verb. A correct sentence would be, "I should have gone to bed."

20. **All of the following are true about a descriptive essay EXCEPT:**
(Average)

A. Its purpose is to make an experience available through one of the five senses

B. Its words make it possible for the reader to see with their mind's eye

C. Its language will move people because of the emotion involved

D. It is not trying to get anyone to take a certain action

Answer: D. It is not trying to get anyone to take a certain action
The descriptive essay uses language to make an experience available to readers. It uses descriptive words so the reader can see with their mind's eye, smell with their mind's nose, etc. Descriptive writing will involve the emotions of both the reader and writer. Poems are excellent examples of descriptive writing. An exposition is the type of essay that is not interested in getting anyone to take a certain action.

21. **A student has written a paper with the following characteristics: written in first person; characters, setting, and plot; some dialogue; events organized in chronological sequence with some flashbacks. In what genre has the student written?**
(Rigorous)

A. Expository writing

B. Narrative writing

C. Persuasive writing

D. Descriptive writing

Answer: B. Narrative writing
These are all characteristics of narrative writing. Expository writing is intended to give information such as an explanation or directions, and the information is logically organized. Persuasive writing gives an opinion in an attempt to convince the reader that this point of view is valid or tries to persuade the reader to take a specific action. The goal of technical writing is to clearly communicate a select piece of information to a targeted reader or group of readers for a particular purpose in such a way that the subject can readily be understood. It is persuasive writing that anticipates a response from the reader.

22. All of the following are stages of the writing process EXCEPT:
(Average)

A. Prewriting

B. Revising

C. Organizing

D. Presenting

Answer: D. Presenting
Writing is a process that can be clearly defined. First, students must prewrite to discover ideas, materials, experiences, sources, etc. Next, they must organize and determine their purpose, thesis, and supporting details. Last, they must edit and revise to polish the paper. While presenting is a nice finale to the writing process, it is not necessary for a complete and polished work.

23. Which of the following should not be included in the opening paragraph of an informative essay?
(Average)

A. Thesis sentence

B. Details and examples supporting the main idea

C. Broad general introduction to the topic

D. A style and tone that grabs the reader's attention

Answer B. Details and examples supporting the main idea
The introductory paragraph should introduce the topic, capture the reader's interest, state the thesis, and prepare the reader for the main points in the essay. Details and examples, however, should be given in the second part of the essay, so as to help develop the thesis presented at the end of the introductory paragraph, following the inverted triangle method consisting of a broad general statement followed by some information, and then the thesis at the end of the paragraph.

24. A sentence that contains one independent clause and three dependent clauses best describes a:
(Average)

A. Simple sentence

B. Compound sentence

C. Complex sentence

D. Compound-complex sentence

Answer: C. Complex Sentence
A complex sentence is made up of one independent clause and at least one dependent clause. This type of sentence can have multiple dependent clauses in it. Simple and compound sentences will not have any dependent clauses, and a compound-complex sentence will have more than one independent clause as well as one or more dependent clauses.

25. The main idea of a paragraph or story:
(Average)

A. Is what the paragraph or story is about

B. Indicates what the passage is about

C. Gives more information about the topic

D. States the important ideas that the author wants the reader to know about a topic

Answer: D. States the important ideas that the author wants the reader to know about a topic.
The main idea of a paragraph or story states the important ideas that the author wants the reader to know about his/her topic. The main idea can be directly stated or simply implied. The topic is what the paragraph or story is about. A topic sentence will indicate what a specific passage is about. And supporting details will give more information about a topic.

26. A strong topic sentence will:
(Rigorous)

A. Be phrased as a question.

B. Always be the first sentence in a paragraph.

C. Both A and B

D. Neither A nor B

Answer: D Neither A nor B
A topic sentence will tell what the passage is about. A tip for finding a topic sentence is to phrase the possible topic sentence as a question and see if the other sentences answer the question, but the topic sentence doesn't need to be in question form. A topic sentence is usually the first sentence in a paragraph but could also be in any other position. Therefore neither choices A nor B are correct choices.

27. Which of the following is a great way to keep a natural atmosphere when speaking publicly?
(Average)

A. Speak slowly

B. Maintain a straight, but not stiff, posture

C. Use friendly gestures

D. Take a step to the side every once in a while

Answer: C. Use friendly gestures.
Gestures are a great way to keep a natural atmosphere when speaking publicly. Gestures that are common in friendly conversation will make the audience feel at ease. Gestures that are exaggerated, stiff, or awkward will only distract from a speech. Speaking slowly, monitoring posture, and taking a step to the side are great speaking skills but not skills that will create a natural atmosphere.

28. Students returning from a field trip to the local newspaper want to thank their hosts for the guided tour. As their teacher, what form of communication should you encourage them to use?
(Rigorous)

A. Each student will send an e-mail expressing his or her appreciation

B. As a class, students will create a blog, and each student will write about what they learned

C. Each student will write a thank you letter that the teacher will fax to the newspaper

D. Each student will write a thank you note that the teacher will mail to the newspaper.

Answer: D. Each student will write a thank you note that the teacher will mail to the newspaper
Courtesy requires a hand-written message that is brief and specific. While using technology such as e-mails, blogs, and faxes are quicker, they are less personal. Communication channels and language styles vary; teachers should model correct behavior and appropriate uses of communication.

29. **Which of the following skills can help students improve their listening comprehension?**
(Rigorous)

I. Tap into prior knowledge.
II. Look for transitions between ideas.
III. Ask questions of the speaker.
IV. Discuss the topic being presented.

A. I and II only

B. II and IV only

C. II and IV only

D. IV only

Answer: A. I and II only
Many strategies that are effective in improving reading comprehension are also effective in improving listening comprehension. Tapping into prior knowledge and looking for transitions between ideas are excellent listening and reading comprehension strategies. Asking questions of the speaker may help clarify ideas and discussing the topic may help organize the thoughts being presented, but both are difficult to do during the actual act of listening.

30. As Ms. Wolmark looks at the mandated vocabulary curriculum for the 5th grade, she notes that she can opt to teach foreign words and abbreviations which have become part of the English language. She decides:
(Rigorous)

A. To forego that since she is not a teacher of foreign language

B. To teach only foreign words from the native language of her four ELL students

C. To use the ELL students' native languages as a start for an extensive study of foreign language words

D. To teach 2-3 foreign language words that are now in English and let it go at that

Answer: C. To use the ELL students' native languages as a start for an extensive study of foreign language words
Incorporating the native language of ELL students into instruction helps to form a bond between their native language and English. It also serves as a point of confidence that connects that student with the other students in the class.

Answer Key: Reading

1. A
2. A
3. C
4. B
5. B
6. B
7. B
8. D
9. A
10. C
11. A
12. A
13. C
14. C
15. C
16. C
17. C
18. D
19. B
20. D
21. B
22. D
23. B
24. C
25. D
26. D
27. C
28. D
29. A
30. C

Rigor Table: Reading

	Easy 0%	Average 60%	Rigorous 40%
Questions		**1, 4, 5, 6, 7, 9, 12, 13, 14, 16, 18, 20, 21, 22, 23, 24, 25, 27**	**2, 3, 8, 10, 11, 15, 17, 19, 26, 28, ,29, 30**

MATH

1. **A truck rental company charges $40 per day plus $2.50 per mile. The odometer reading is M miles when a customer rents a truck and m miles when it is returned d days later. Which expression represents the total charge for the rental?**
(Rigorous)

A. $40d + 2.5M - m$

B. $40d + 2.5m - M$

C. $40d + 2.5(M - m)$

D. $40d + 2.5(m - M)$

Answer: D. $40d + 2.5(m - M)$
Rental for d days is $40d$. The number of miles driven is $m - M$. The charge for miles driven is $2.50(m - M)$. Beginning mileage must be subtracted from ending mileage and the *difference* multiplied by 2.5.

2. **Using a pattern is an appropriate strategy for which of the following:**

I. Skip counting
II. Counting backward
III. Finding doubles

(Easy)

A. I and II

B. I and III

C. II and III

D. I, II, and III

Answer: A. I and II
The skip-counting pattern adds the same number repeatedly. Counting backward subtracts 1 repeatedly.

3. **The following set of numbers is not closed under addition:**
(Rigorous)

A. Set of all real numbers

B. Set of all even numbers

C. Set of all odd numbers

D. Set of all rational numbers

Answer: C. Set of all odd numbers
Adding two real numbers will result in a real number. The same is true for even or rational numbers. Adding two odd numbers, however, will not always produce an odd number.

4. **What is the value of the following expression?**

$$\frac{25-2(6-2\bullet 3)}{{}^{-}5(2+2\bullet 4)}$$

(Rigorous)

A. 0.5

B. 5.0

C. -0.5

D. 3.4

Answer: C. –0.5
The fraction line is equivalent to parentheses and indicates that the numerator is to be simplified first. Then use the standard order of operations.

$$\frac{25-2(6-2\bullet 3)}{{}^{-}5(2+2\bullet 4)}=\frac{25-2(6-6)}{-5(2+8)}=\frac{25-0}{-5(10)}=\frac{25}{-50}=-0.5$$

5. **Which of the following expressions are equivalent to 28 – 4 • 6 +12?**

I.	**(28 – 4) • 6 +12**
II.	**28 – (4 • 6) +12**
III.	**(28 – 4) • (6 +12)**
IV.	**(28 + 12) – (4 • 6)**
V.	**28 – 4 • 12 + 6**

(Average)

A. I and V

B. II and IV

C. III and V

D. IV and V

Answer: B. II and IV
The parentheses in expression II indicate that the multiplication is to be done first. Using the standard order of operations: multiply and divide from left to right, then add and subtract from left to right.

6. **If *n* represents an odd number, which of the following does not represent an even number?**
(Average)

A. $2n$

B. $2(n + 1)$

C. n^2

D. $10n - 2$

Answer: C. n^2
n^2 represents an odd number times an odd number, which will be an odd number. Choices A, B, and D are multiples of 2 and represent even numbers.

7. **Based upon the following examples, can you conclude that the sum of two prime numbers is also a prime number? Why or why not?**

$$2 + 3 = 5$$
$$2 + 5 = 7$$
$$11 + 2 = 13$$

(Rigorous)

A. Yes; there is a pattern

B. Yes; there are many more examples, such as 17 + 2 = 19 and 29 + 2 = 31

C. No; there are many counterexamples

D. No; the sums are not prime numbers

Answer: C. No; there are many counterexamples
Only one counterexample is needed to disprove a statement. For example, in 3 + 5 = 8 the sum is a composite number. Care must be taken not to generalize a perceived pattern based upon too few examples. Additional examples are not sufficient to establish a pattern. In choice D, 5, 7, and 13 are prime numbers.

8. **If *x* is a whole number, what is the best description of the number 4*x* + 1? *(Rigorous)***

A. Prime number

B. Composite number

C. Odd number

D. Even number

Answer: C. Odd number
Since 4*x* is a multiple of 4, it is an even number. One more than an even number is an odd number. The prime numbers do not follow a pattern. 4*x* + 1 may be either prime, for example 13, or composite, for example 9.

9. The plot for a proposed new city hall plaza is 120 feet long by 90 feet wide. A scale model for the plaza must fit in an area that is 10 feet square. If the largest possible model is built in that area, what will be the maximum possible width for the scale model?
(Rigorous)

A. $\frac{2}{15}$ ft

B. $1\frac{1}{3}$ ft

C. $7\frac{1}{2}$ ft

D. $13\frac{1}{3}$ ft

Answer: C $7\frac{1}{2}$ **ft**

Use a proportion to find the maximum width:

$$\frac{120}{10} = \frac{90}{x} \rightarrow x = 7\frac{1}{2}$$

The maximum width is $7\frac{1}{2}$ ft. Be sure to set up the proportion with equivalent ratios to find the maximum width. Check for reasonableness of results. The width cannot exceed 10 ft.

10. Jocelyn wants create a magnetic board in the back of her classroom by covering part of the wall with a special magnetic paint. Each can of paint will cover 15 square feet. If the area is 12 feet wide and 8 feet high, how many cans of paint should she buy?
(Average)

A. 5 cans

B. 6 cans

C. 7 cans

D. 8 cans

Answer: C. 7 cans
First, find the area of the magnetic board. Then divide by 15.

$$12 \times 8 = 96$$
$$96 \div 15 = 6.4$$

Jocelyn cannot buy 6.4 cans. She must buy 7 cans. Consider the meaning of any remainder in the context of the problem.

11. A recipe makes 6 servings and calls for $1\frac{1}{2}$ cups of rice. How much rice is needed to make 10 servings?
(Average)

A. 2 cups

B. $2\frac{1}{4}$ cups

C. $2\frac{1}{2}$ cups

D. $2\frac{3}{4}$ cups

Answer: C. $2\frac{1}{2}$ cups

Write and solve a proportion.

$$\frac{1.5}{6} = \frac{x}{10}$$
$$1.5(10) = 6x$$
$$x = 2.5$$

When writing a proportion, check that the ratios are equivalent:

$$\frac{\text{cups of rice}}{\text{servings}} = \frac{\text{cups of rice}}{\text{servings}}$$

12. Which table(s) represents solutions of the following equation?

$$2x - 5y = 50$$

I

x	$^{-}5$	0	5	10
y	$^{-}12$	$^{-}10$	$^{-}8$	$^{-}6$

II

x	$^{-}5$	0	5	$^{-}10$
y	$^{-}12$	$^{-}10$	$^{-}12$	$^{-}10$

III

x	20	25	30	35
y	$^{-}2$	0	2	4

(Rigorous)

A. I

B. II

C. II and III

D. I and III

Answer: D. I and III

Substitute values for *x* and *y* into the equation. For example, if $x = {}^{-}5$ and $y = {}^{-}12$, then

$$2({}^{-}5) - 5({}^{-}12) = 50$$
$$^{-}10 - ({}^{-}60) = 50$$
$$^{-}10 + 60 = 50$$

Since the equation is true, the values $x = {}^{-}5$ and $y = {}^{-}12$ are solutions of the equation.
In table II, substituting the values $x = 5$ and $y = {}^{-}12$, gives a false statement since

$$2(5) - 5({}^{-}12) = 50$$
$$10 - ({}^{-}60) = 50$$
$$10 + 60 = 50$$

13. The relations given below demonstrate the following addition and multiplication property of real numbers:

a + b = b + a
ab = ba

(Average)

A. Commutative

B. Associative

C. Identity

D. Inverse

Answer: A. Commutative
Both addition and multiplication of real numbers satisfy the commutative property, according to which changing the order of the operands does not change the result of the operation.

14 Which property (or properties) is applied below?

$$^{-}8x + 5x = (^{-}8 + 5)x$$
$$= {}^{-}3x$$

I. Associative Property of Addition
II. Zero Property of Addition
III. Additive Inverses
IV. Identity Property of Multiplication
V. Distributive Property

(Rigorous)

A. I

B. V

C. I and III

D. II and IV

Answer: B. V
The variable *x* is distributed over the sum of $^{-}8$ and 5. Check definitions of properties.

15. For which of the following is the additive inverse equal to the multiplicative inverse?
(Rigorous)

A. $\frac{2}{3}+\frac{3}{2}$

B. $\sqrt{-1}$

C. $\frac{1-\sqrt{2}}{1+\sqrt{2}}$

D. $(a+b)/(b-a)$

Answer: B. $\sqrt{-1}$

Let the number for which the additive inverse is equal to the multiplicative inverse be x. Then $-x=\frac{1}{x}; \Rightarrow x^2=-1; x=\sqrt{-1}$

16. Which of the statements below explain the error(s), if any, in the following calculation?

$$\frac{18}{18} + 23 = 23$$

I. A number divided by itself is 1, not 0.
II. The sum of 1 and 23 is 24, not 23.
III. The 18s are "cancelled" and replaced by 0.

(Rigorous)

A. I and II

B. II and III

C. I, II, and III

D. There is no error.

Answer: C. I, II, and III

$\frac{18}{18} = 1$ and 1 + 23 = 24

17. Which statement is a model for the following problem?

27 less than 5 times a number is 193.

(Average)

A. $27 < 5x + 193$

B. $27 - 5x < 193$

C. $5x - 27 < 193$

D. $5x - 27 = 193$

Answer: D. $5x - 27 = 193$

5 times a number is represented by $5x$; 27 less than $5x$ by $5x - 27$; the difference *is* (equals) 193, not *is less than* 193. Avoid confusing *is less than* with *less than.*

18. What is the solution set of the following inequality?

$$\mathbf{4x + 9 \geq 11(x - 3)}$$

(Average)

A. $x \leq 0$

B. $x \geq 0$

C. $x \leq 6$

D. $x \geq 6$

Answer: C. $x \leq 6$
Apply the distributive property on the right.

$$4x + 9 \geq 11(x - 3)$$
$$4x + 9 \geq 11x - 33$$
$$11x - 4x \leq 9 + 33$$
$$7x \leq 42$$
$$x \leq 6$$

19. A car is rented in Quebec. The outside temperature shown on the dashboard reads 17°C. What is the temperature in degrees Fahrenheit? (Use the formula $F = \frac{9}{5}C + 32$.)

(Average)

A. 27.2°*F*

B. 41.4°*F*

C. 62.6°*F*

D. 88.2°*F*

Answer: C 62.6°*F*

Use the order of operations. First multiply $\frac{9}{5}$ and 17. Then add 32 to the result.

$$F = (\frac{9}{5} \cdot 17) + 32$$
$$= 30.6 + 32$$
$$= 62.6$$

20. The two solutions of the quadratic equation $ax^2 + bx + c = 0$ are given by the formula $x = \frac{-b \pm \sqrt{b^2 - 4ac}}{2a}$. What are the solutions of the equation $x^2 - 18x + 32$?
(Rigorous)

A. $^-5$ and 23

B. 2 and 16

C. $9 \pm \sqrt{113}$

D. $9 \pm 2\sqrt{113}$

Answer: B. 2 and 16

Substitute in the formula: a = 1, b = $^-18$, c = 32: $x = \frac{18 \pm \sqrt{18^2 - 4(32)}}{2}$. Then apply the standard order of operations: $x = \frac{18+14}{2}$ and $x = \frac{18-14}{2}$, or x = 16 and x = 2. Be sure to apply the standard order of operations after substituting in the formula.

21. **Triangle *ABC* is rotated 90° clockwise about the origin and translated 6 units left.**

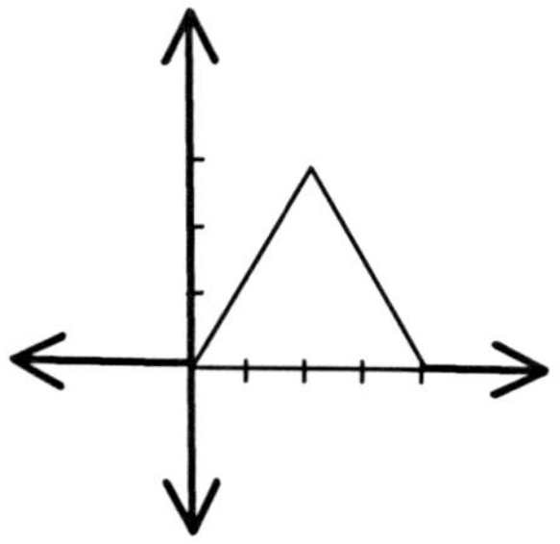

What are the coordinates of *B* after the transformations?
(Rigorous)

A. (2, ¯3)

B. (3, ¯2)

C. (¯2, ¯3)

D. (¯3, ¯2)

Answer: D. (¯3, ¯2)
Under the rotation, (2, 3) → (3, ¯2). Sliding 6 units left, (3, ¯2) → (¯3, ¯2). Work with one transformation at a time, rather than trying to do both at the same time.

22. The following represents the net of a

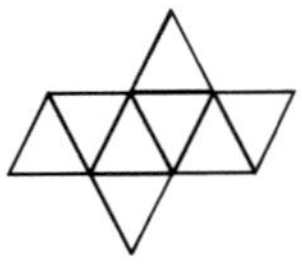

(Average)

A. Cube

B. Tetrahedron

C. Octahedron

D. Dodecahedron

Answer: C. Octahedron
The eight equilateral triangles make up the eight faces of an octahedron.

23. Ginny and Nick head back to their respective colleges after being home for the weekend. They leave their house at the same time and drive for 4 hours. Ginny drives due south at the average rate of 60 miles per hour and Nick drives due east at the average rate of 60 miles per hour. What is the straight-line distance between them, in miles, at the end of the 4 hours? *(Rigorous)*

A. 169.7 miles

B. 240 miles

C. 288 miles

D. 339.4 miles

Answer: D. 339.4 miles

Ginny and Nick each drive a distance of 4 × 60, or 240 miles. Draw a diagram.

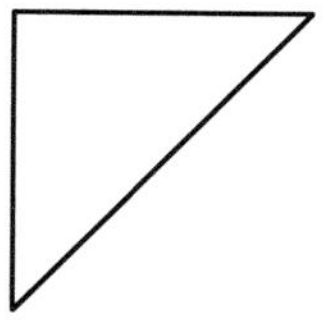

Then apply the Pythagorean Theorem: $c^2 = a^2 + b^2$.

$$\begin{aligned} x^2 &= 240^2 + 240^2 \\ &= 115,200 \\ x &= \sqrt{115,200} \\ x &\approx 339.4 \end{aligned}$$

So x is about 339.4 miles. Be sure to use the standard order of operations when solving for x.

24. What is the surface area of the prism shown below?
(Rigorous)

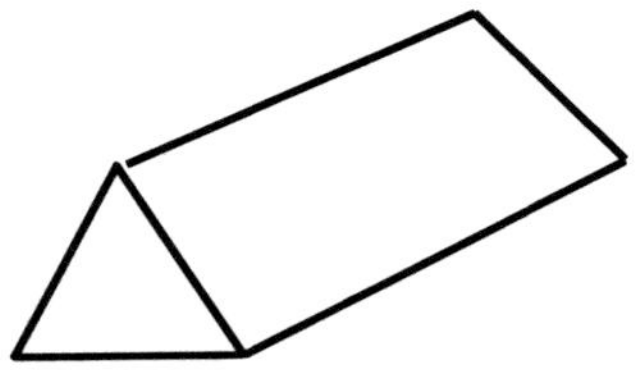

A. 204 cm^2

B. 216 cm^2

C. 360 cm^2

D. 180 cm^2

Answer: B. 216 cm
Find the area of each face. Each triangular face has an altitude of 4 cm and area of 12 cm^2. Surface area = 5(12) + 5(12) + 6(12) + 12 + 12, which equals 216. Check that the areas of all the faces are included in the sum, especially the bottom and the back of the prism.

25. **Which of the following is not equivalent to 3 km?**

I. 3.0×10^3 m
II. 3.0×10^4 cm
III. 3.0×10^6 mm

(Average)

A. I

B. II

C. III

D. None of the above

Answer: B. II
There are 1000, or 103 meters in each kilometer; 100, or 10^2 cm, in each meter; and 10 millimeters in each centimeter. Remember to add exponents when multiplying: for example, 3.0×10^3 m = $3.0 \times 10^3 \times 10^2$ cm, or 3.0×10^5 cm.

26. **A school band has 200 members. Looking at the pie chart below, determine which statement is true about the band.**

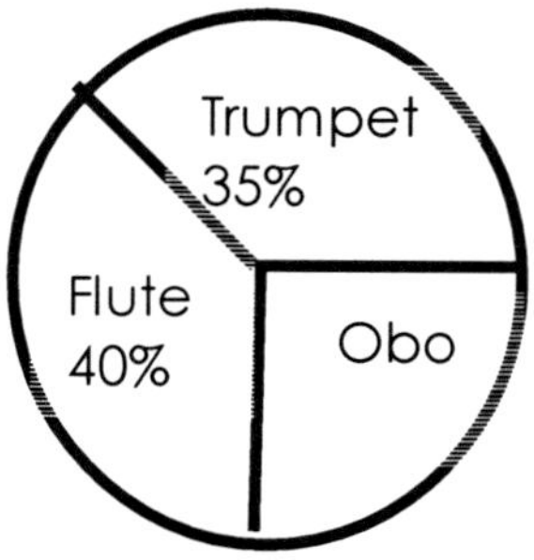

(Average)

A. There are more trumpet players than flute players

B. There are fifty oboe players in the band

C. There are forty flute players in the band

D. One-third of all band members play the trumpet

Answer: B. There are fifty oboe players in the band
There are fifty oboe players in the band since 25% of 200 is 50.

27. A restaurant offers the following menu choices.

Green Vegetable	Yellow Vegetable
Asparagus	Carrots
Broccoli	Corn
Peas	Squash
Spinach	

If a customer chooses a green vegetable and a yellow vegetable at random, what is the probability that the customer will order neither asparagus nor corn?
(Rigorous)

A. $\frac{1}{12}$

B. $\frac{1}{6}$

C. $\frac{1}{3}$

D. $\frac{1}{2}$

Answer: D
There are 4 × 3, or 12 possible combinations of choices. Of those, 6 include either asparagus or corn or both (1 asparagus and corn, 2 asparagus and not corn, and 3 corn but not asparagus). Since 6 out of the 12 choices are favorable, the probability is $\frac{6}{12}$, or $\frac{1}{2}$. Be careful not to count any choice (asparagus and corn) more than once.

28. A school has 15 male teachers and 35 female teachers. In how many ways can they form a committee with 2 male teachers and 4 female teachers on it?
(Average)

A. 525

B. 5497800

C. 88

D. 263894400

Answer: B. 5497800
The number of ways one can pick 2 male teachers out of 15 =

$$^{15}_{2}C = \frac{15!}{13!2!} = \frac{14x15}{2} = 105$$

The number of ways one can pick 4 female teachers out of 35 =

$$^{35}_{4}C = \frac{35!}{31!4!} = \frac{32x33x34x35}{2x3x4} = 52360$$

Hence, the total number of ways the committee can be chosen = 105 x 52360 = 5497800.

29. A music store owner wants to change the window display every week. Only 4 out of 6 instruments can be displayed in the window at the same time. How many weeks will it be before the owner must repeat the same arrangement (in the same order) of instruments in the window display?
(Rigorous)

A. 24 weeks

B. 36 weeks

C. 120 weeks

D. 360 weeks

Answer: D. 360 weeks
There are 6 choices for the first position. For each of those choices, there are 5 choices for the second position and 6 × 5 choices for the first two positions. For each of those there are 3 choices for the third position and 2 for the fourth position: 6 × 5 × 4 × 3 = 360.

30. Half the students in a class scored 80% on an exam; one student scored 10%; and the rest of the class scored 85%. Which would be the best measure of central tendency for the test scores?
(Rigorous)

A. Mean

B. Median

C. Mode

D. Either the median or the mode because they are equal

Answer: B
The median is the least sensitive to extreme values. The mode reports only one score and is not a reflection of the entire data set. The mean will be skewed by the outlier of 10%.

Answer Key: Math

1. D
2. A
3. C
4. C
5. B
6. C
7. C
8. C
9. C
10. C
11. C
12. D
13. A
14. B
15. B
16. C
17. C
18. C
19. C
20. B
21. D
22. C
23. D
24. B
25. B
26. B
27. D
28. B
29. D
30. B

Rigor Table: Math

	Easy 3.3%	Average 40%	Rigorous 56.7%
Questions	**2**	**5, 6, 10, 11, 13, 17, 18, 19, 22, 25, 26, 28**	**1, 3, 4, 7, 8, 9, 12, 14, 15, 16, 20, 21, 23, 24, 27, 29, 30**

SOCIAL SCIENCES

1. The Great Plains in the United States are an excellent place to grow corn and wheat for all of the following reasons EXCEPT:
(Average)

A. Rainfall is abundant and the soil is rich

B. The land is mostly flat and easy to cultivate

C. The human population is modest in size, so there is plenty of space for large farms

D. The climate is semitropical

Answer: D. The climate is semitropical
The climate on the Great Plains is not semitropical. It is temperate, with harsh winters. Rainfall and soil conditions are good. The land is flat. The human population is not overcrowded; there is room for large farms.

2. What is characteristic of areas of the world with high populations?
(Rigorous)

A. These areas tend to have heavy pollution

B. These areas are almost always surrounded by suburbs

C. Populations are rarely located near one another

D. Most populated places in the world also tend to be close to agricultural lands

Answer: D. Most populated places in the world also tend to be close to agricultural lands.
Pollution (choice A) and suburbs (choice B) are often found in populated areas, but they are not always present and are not mentioned in the text. The text says that population centers are often, not rarely (choice C), located near each other.

3. Meridians, or lines of longitude, not only help in pinpointing locations but are also used for:
(Average)

A. Measuring distance from the Poles

B. Determining direction of ocean currents

C. Determining the time around the world

D. Measuring distance on the equator

Answer: C. Determining the time around the world
Meridians, or lines of longitude, are the determining factor in separating time zones and determining time around the world.

4. The Western Hemisphere contains all of which of the following continents?
(Rigorous)

A. Russia

B. Europe

C. North America

D. Asia

Answer: C North America
The Western Hemisphere, located between the North and South Poles and between the Prime Meridian (0 degrees longitude) west to the International Date Line at 180 degrees longitude, consists of all of North and South America, a tiny part of the easternmost part of Russia that extends east of 180 degrees longitude, and a part of Europe that extends west of the Prime Meridian (0 degrees longitude).

5. **Mr. Allen is discussing the earthquake in Chile and explains the aftershocks and tsunamis that threatened Pacific islands thousands of miles away. What aspect of geographical studies was he emphasizing?**
(Rigorous)

A. Regional

B. Topical

C. Physical

D. Human

Answer: C. Physical
Earthquakes, aftershocks, and tsunamis are physical features on the earth. Regional studies would focus on the elements or characteristics of a particular region, such as in Chile itself. Topical studies focus on an earth feature or human activity occurring throughout the entire world, such as talking about earthquakes in Italy, Haiti, Chile, Mexico and other countries. Human studies would focus on human activity patterns and how they relate to the environment including political, cultural, historical, urban, and social geographical fields of study.

6. **Which of the following are non-renewable resources?**
(Average)

A. Fish, coffee, and forests

B. Fruit, water, and solar energy

C. Wind power, alcohol, and sugar

D. Coal, natural gas, and oil

Answer: D. Coal, natural gas, and oil
Coal, natural gas, and oil are fossil fuels, which cannot be renewed. Nonrenewable resources are natural resources that cannot be remade or regenerated in the same proportion that they are used. Renewable resources are generally living resources (fish, coffee, and forests, for example), which can restock (renew) themselves if they are not over harvested. Renewable resources can restock themselves and be used indefinitely if they are sustained.

7. What people perfected the preservation of dead bodies?
(Average)

A. Sumerians

B. Phoenicians

C. Egyptians

D. Assyrians

Answer: C Egyptians
The Sumerians (choice A), Phoenicians (choice B), and Assyrians (choice D) all made contributions to ancient civilization but preserving dead bodies was not among their respective contributions.

8. Which of these is NOT a true statement about the Roman civilization?
(Rigorous)

A. Its period of Pax Romana provided long periods of peace during which travel and trade increased, enabling the spread of culture, goods, and ideas over the known world

B. It borrowed the concept of democracy from the Greeks and developed it into a complex representative government

C. It flourished in the arts with realistic approach to art and a dramatic use of architecture

D. It developed agricultural innovations such as crop rotation and terrace farming

Answer: D. It developed agricultural innovations such as crop rotation and terrace farming
China developed crop rotation and terrace farming.

9. The major force in eighteenth and nineteenth century politics was:
(Average)

A. Nationalism

B. Revolution

C. War

D. Diplomacy

Answer: A. Nationalism
Nationalism was the driving force in politics in the eighteenth and nineteenth century. Groups of people that shared common traits and characteristics wanted their own government and countries. This led to some revolution, war, and the failure of diplomacy.

10. The identification of individuals or groups as they are influenced by their own group or culture is called:
(Average)

A. Cross-cultural exchanges

B. Cultural diffusion

C. Cultural identity

D. Cosmopolitanism

Answer: C. Cultural identity
Cross-cultural exchanges involved the discovery of shared values and needs as well as an appreciation of differences. Cultural diffusion is the movement of cultural ideas or materials between populations independent of the movement of those populations. Cosmopolitanism blurs cultural differences in the creation of a shared new culture.

11. The New England colonies included:
(Average)

A. South Carolina

B. Georgia

C. Massachusetts

D. New York

Answer: C. Massachusetts
South Carolina (choice A) and Georgia (choice B) were southern colonies. New York (choice D) was a middle Atlantic colony.

12. Which major economic activity of the Southern colonies led to the growth of slavery?
(Rigorous)

A. Manufacturing

B. Fishing

C. Farming

D. Coal mining

Answer: C. Farming
The major economic activity in this region was farming. Here the soil was very fertile, and the climate was very mild with an even longer growing season than farther north. The large plantations, eventually requiring large numbers of slaves, were found in the coastal or tidewater areas. Although the wealthy slave-owning planters set the pattern of life in this region, most of the people lived inland away from coastal areas. They were small farmers and very few, if any, owned slaves.

13. Which was the first instance of an internal tax on the American colonies?
(Average)

A. The Proclamation Act

B. The Sugar Act

C. The Currency Act

D. The Stamp Act

Answer: D. The Stamp Act
The Proclamation Act prohibited English settlement beyond the Appalachian Mountains to appease the Native Americans. The Sugar Act imposed a tax on foreign molasses, sugar, and other goods imported into the colonies. The Currency Act prohibited colonial governments from issuing paper money. The Stamp Act placed a tax on newspapers, legal documents, licenses, almanacs, and playing cards which made it the first instance of an "internal" tax on the colonies.

14. The Lewis and Clark expedition advanced knowledge in each of the following areas except:
(Average)

A. Geography

B. Modern warfare

C. Botany

D. Animal life

Answer: B. Modern warfare
The Lewis and Clark expedition was peaceful. Lewis and Clark learned a great deal about geography, botany, and animal life.

15. Populism arises out of a feeling:
(Average)

A. Of intense happiness

B. Of satisfaction with the activities of large corporations

C. That women should not be allowed to vote

D. Perceived oppression

Answer: D Perceived oppression
Perceived oppression felt by average people toward the wealthy elite gave rise to Populism. Populists do not become prominent when people are happy (choice A), or when people are satisfied with the activities of large corporations (choice B). Populists and other progressives fought for, not against (choice C), voting rights for women.

16. At the end of the Twentieth Century, the United States was:
(Average)

A. A central leader in international affairs

B. A reluctant participant in international affairs

C. One of two superpowers

D. Lacking a large consumer culture

Answer: A. A central leader in international affairs
It was a reluctant participant (choice B) in international affairs at the beginning of the twentieth century. The United States was the only superpower (choice C) left at the end of the twentieth century. The United States developed a large consumer culture (choice D) in the 1950s and still has it today.

17. How did manufacturing change in the early 1800s?
(Rigorous)

A. The electronics industry was born

B. Production moved from small shops or homes into factories

C. Industry benefited from the Federal Reserve Act

D. The timber industry was hurt when Theodore Roosevelt set aside 238 million acres of federal lands to be protected from development

Answer: B. Production moved from small shops or homes into factories
Factories had modern machinery in them that could produce goods efficiently. The electronics industry (choice A) did not exist in the early 1800s. The Federal Reserve Act (choice C) came much later, in the Twentieth Century. Theodore Roosevelt's protection of federal lands from development (choice D) also took place in the Twentieth Century.

18. The early ancient civilizations developed systems of government:
(Rigorous)

A. To provide for defense against attack

B. To regulate trade

C. To regulate and direct the economic activities of the people as they worked together in groups

D. To decide on the boundaries of the different fields during planting seasons

Answer: C. To regulate and direct the economic activities of the people as they worked together in groups
Although ancient civilizations were concerned with defense, trade regulation, and the maintenance of boundaries in their fields, they could not have done any of them without first regulating and directing the economic activities of the people as they worked in groups. This provided for a stable economic base from which they could trade and actually had something worth providing defense for.

19. What is another name for dictatorship?
(Rigorous)

A. Oligarchy

B. Monarchy

C. Anarchism

D. Communism

Answer: A. Oligarchy
Monarchy (choice B) features a king or a queen, not a dictator. Anarchism (choice C) favors the elimination of all government and its replacement by a cooperative community of individuals. Dictatorship is not about cooperating between individuals. Communism (choice D) is decentralized, while dictatorship is highly centralized.

20. Which of the following documents described and defined the system and structure of the United States government?
(Average)

A. The Bill of Rights

B. The Declaration of Independence

C. The Constitution

D. The Articles of Confederation

Answer: C. The Constitution
The United States Constitution is the written document that describes and defines the system and structure of the United States government. The first ten Amendments to the Constitution are called the Bill of Rights. The Declaration of Independence, written in 1776 by Thomas Jefferson, was a call to the colonies to unite against the King, detailing the grievances of the colonies and articulating the philosophical framework upon which the United States is founded. The Articles of Confederation were the first attempt of the newly independent states to reach a new understanding among themselves.

21. How did the ideology of John Locke influence Thomas Jefferson in writing the Declaration of Independence?
(Rigorous)

A. Locke emphasized human rights and believed that people should rebel against governments who violated those rights

B. Locke emphasized the rights of government to protect its people and to levy taxes

C. Locke believed in the British system of monarchy and the rights of Parliament to make laws

D. Locke advocated individual rights over the collective whole

Answer: A. Locke emphasized human rights and believed that people should rebel against governments who violated those rights
The Declaration of Independence is an outgrowth of both ancient Greek ideas of democracy and individual rights and the ideas of the European Enlightenment and the Renaissance, especially the ideology of the political thinker John Locke. Thomas Jefferson (1743–1826) the principle author of the Declaration borrowed much from Locke's theories and writings. John Locke was one of the most influential political writers of the seventeenth century who put great emphasis on human rights and put forth the belief that when governments violate those rights people should rebel. He wrote the book *Two Treatises of Government* in 1690, which had tremendous influence on political thought in the American colonies and helped shape the U.S. Constitution and Declaration of Independence.

22. Which of the following is not a right declared by the U.S. Constitution? *(Average)*

A. The right to speak out in public

B. The right to use cruel and unusual punishment

C. The right to a speedy trial

D. The right not to be forced to testify against yourself

Answer: B The right to use cruel and unusual punishment.
A person who lives in a democratic society legally has a comprehensive list of rights guaranteed to him or her by the government. In the United States, this is the Constitution and its Amendments. Among these very important rights are:

- the right to speak out in public;
- the right to pursue any religion;
- the right for a group of people to gather in public for any reason that doesn't fall under a national security cloud;
- the right not to have soldiers stationed in your home;
- the right not to be forced to testify against yourself in a court of law;
- the right to a speedy and public trial by a jury of your peers;
- the right not to be the victim of cruel and unusual punishment; and
- the right to avoid unreasonable search and seizure of your person, your house, and your vehicle.

23. The cold weather froze orange crops in Florida and the price of orange juice increased. This is an example of what economic concept? *(Rigorous)*

A. Output market

B. Input market

C. Supply and demand

D. Entrepreneurship

Answer: C. Supply and demand.
Output markets refer to the market in which goods and services are sold. The *input market* is the market in which factors of production, or resources, are bought and sold.

24. What type of production process must producers choose?
(Average)

A. One that is inefficient

B. One that often produces goods that consumers don't want

C. One that is efficient

D. One that is sometimes efficient and sometimes inefficient

Answer: C. One that is efficient.
Producers cannot stay in business if they operate inefficiently (choice A). Producers cannot afford to produce goods that consumers don't want (choice B). Producers will suffer if their efficiency is inconsistent (choice D).

25. The existence of economics is based on:
(Rigorous)

A. The scarcity of resources

B. The abundance of resources

C. Little or nothing that is related to resources

D. Entrepreneurship

Answer: A. The scarcity of resources.
If resources were always abundant (choice B), economics would be unnecessary. Economics is closely, not loosely (choice C) related to resources. Entrepreneurship (choice D) is part of economics, but is not the primary basis of economics.

26. In the fictional country of Nacirema, the government controls the means of production and directs resources. It alone decides what will be produced; as a result, there is an abundance of capital and military goods but a scarcity of consumer goods. What type of economy is this?
(Rigorous)

A. Market economy

B. Centrally planned economy

C. Market socialism

D. Capitalism

Answer: B. Centrally planned economy.
In a planned economy, the means of production are publicly owned, with little, if any private ownership. Instead of the "three questions" being solved by markets, there is a planning authority that makes the decisions. The planning authority decides what will be produced and how. Since most planned economies direct resources into the production of capital and military goods, there is little remaining for consumer goods; the result is often chronic shortages.

27. Which of the following are secondary research materials?
(Average)

A. The conclusions and inferences of other historians

B. Literature and nonverbal materials, novels, stories, poetry, and essays from the period, as well as coins, archaeological artifacts, and art produced during the period

C. Interviews and surveys conducted by the researcher

D. Statistics gathered as the result of the research's experiments

Answer: A. The conclusions and inferences of other historians
Secondary sources are works written significantly after the period being studied and based upon primary sources. In this case, historians have studied artifacts of the time and drawn their conclusion and inferences. Primary sources are the basic materials that provide raw data and information. Students or researchers may use literature and other data they have collected to draw their own conclusions or inferences.

28. For their research paper on the effects of the Civil War on American literature, students have brainstormed a list of potential online sources and are seeking your authorization. Which of these represent the strongest source?
(Rigorous)

A. http://www.wikipedia.org/

B. http://www.google.com

C. http://www.nytimes.com

D. http://docsouth.unc.edu/southlit/civilwar.html

Answer: D. http://docsouth.unc.edu/southlit/civilwar.html
Sites with an "edu" domain are associated with educational institutions and tend to be more trustworthy for research information. Wikipedia has an "org" domain, which means it is a nonprofit. While Wikipedia may be appropriate for background reading, its credibility as a research site is questionable. Both Google and the New York Times are "com" sites, which are for profit. Even though this does not discredit their information, each site is problematic for researchers. With Google, students will get overwhelmed with hits and may not choose the most reputable sites for their information. As a newspaper, the New York Times would not be a strong source for historical information.

29. **For the historian studying ancient Egypt, which of the following would be least useful?**
(Rigorous)

A. The record of an ancient Greek historian on Greek-Egyptian interaction

B. Letters from an Egyptian ruler to his/her regional governors

C. Inscriptions on stele of the Fourteenth Egyptian Dynasty

D. Letters from a nineteenth century Egyptologist to his wife

Answer: D. Letters from a nineteenth century Egyptologist to his wife
Historians use primary sources from the actual time they are studying whenever possible. Ancient Greek records of interaction with Egypt (choice A), letters from an Egyptian ruler to regional governors (choice B), and inscriptions from the Fourteenth Egyptian Dynasty (choice C) are all primary sources created at or near the actual time being studied. Choice D, letters from a nineteenth century Egyptologist, would not be considered primary sources, as they were created thousands of years after the fact and may not actually be about the subject being studied.

30. **Which of the following can be considered the primary goal of social studies?**
(Rigorous)

A. Recalling specific dates and places

B. Identifying and analyzing social links

C. Using contextual clues to identify eras

D. Linking experiments with history

Answer: B. Identifying and analyzing social links
Historic events and social issues cannot be considered only in isolation. People and their actions are connected in many ways, and events are linked through cause and effect over time. Identifying and analyzing these social and historic links is a primary goal of the social sciences. The methods used to analyze social phenomena borrow from several of the social sciences. Interviews, statistical evaluation, observation, and experimentation are just some of the ways that people's opinions and motivations can be measured. From these opinions, larger social beliefs and movements can be interpreted, and events, issues and social problems can be placed in context to provide a fuller view of their importance.

Answer Key: Social Sciences

1. D
2. D
3. C
4. C
5. C
6. D
7. C
8. D
9. A
10. C
11. C
12. C
13. D
14. B
15. D
16. A
17. B
18. C
19. A
20. C
21. A
22. B
23. C
24. C
25. A
26. B
27. A
28. D
29. D
30. B

Rigor Table: Social Sciences

	Easy 0%	**Average 50%**	**Rigorous 50%**
Questions	**0**	**1, 3, 6, 7, 9, 10, 11, 13, 14, 15, 16, 20, 22, 24, 27**	**2, 4, 5, 8, 12, 17, 18, 19, 21, 23, 25, 26, 28, 29, 30**

SCIENCE

1. Which is the correct order for the layers of Earth's atmosphere? *(Easy)*

A. Troposphere, stratosphere, mesosphere, and thermosphere

B. Mesosphere, stratosphere, troposphere, and thermosphere

C. Troposphere, stratosphere, thermosphere, and mesosphere

D. Thermosphere, troposphere, stratosphere, mesosphere

Answer: A. Troposphere, stratosphere, mesosphere, and thermosphere
All weather occurs in the troposphere. There are few clouds in the stratosphere, but weather balloons can float in this region. Air temperatures start to drop in the mesosphere. The coldest spot on Earth is where the mesosphere meets the thermosphere. The thermosphere extends into outer space.

2. Which statement correctly describes the theory of plate tectonics? *(Easy)*

A. There eight major plates and many small plates that move at a rate of 10 to 50 millimeters per year

B. There is one plate for each continent and they move at a speed too small to measure

C. There are thousands of plates that move 1 to 5 meters per year

D. Earthquakes are caused by the collision of plates

Answer: A. There eight major plates and many small plates that move at a rate of 10 to 50 millimeters meters per year
The motion of plates explains, not only earthquakes, but also mountain building, and the creation of volcanoes. The speed is measureable because there are ways to determine the time it took the plates to move from one position on Earth's surface to another.

3. What type of rock can be classified by the size of the crystals in the rock? *(Easy)*

A. Metamorphic

B. Igneous

C. Minerals

D. Sedimentary

Answer: B. Igneous
Igneous rock is formed when molten rock material cools. It is characterized by its grain size and mineral content. Metamorphic rocks are formed from other rocks as a result of heat and pressure. Sedimentary rocks come from weathering and erosion of pre existing rocks.

4. What are solids with a definite chemical composition and a tendency to split along planes of weakness?
(Easy)

A. Ores

B. Rocks

C. Minerals

D. Salts

Answer: C. Minerals
Rocks are made up of minerals, and ores are rocks than can be processed for a commercial use. Salts are ionic compounds formed from acids and bases.

5. In which of the following eras did life appear?
(Easy)

A. Paleozoic

B. Mesozoic

C. Cenozoic

D. Precambrian

Answer: D. Precambrian
The Cambrian explosion, the rapid appearance of most groups of complex organisms, took place in the Cambrian period, which is part of the Paleozoic era. Humans evolved in the Cenozoic era, dinosaurs in the Mesozoic era, and fish in the Paleozoic era.

6. The use of radioactivity to determine the age of rocks and fossils is called which of the following?
(Easy)

A. Carbon dating

B. Absolute dating

C. Stratigraphy

D. Geological dating

Answer: B. Absolute dating
Carbon dating measures the relative amount of carbon-14, which is radioactive, with the amount of carbon-12. The ratio of carbon-12 and carbon-14 in an organic substance at different points in time is known. Stratigraphy is the study or rock layers.

7. Which of the following astronomical entities is not part of the galaxy the Sun is located in?
(Easy)

A. Nebulae

B. Quasars

C. Pulsars

D. Neutron stars

Answer: B. Quasars
Nebulae are visible in the night sky and are glowing clouds of dust, hydrogen, and plasma. Neutron stars are the remnants of super novae, and pulsars are neutron stars that emit radio waves on a periodic basis. A quasar is a distant galaxy that emits large amounts of visible light and radio waves.

8. Why is the winter in the southern hemisphere colder than winter in the northern hemisphere?
(Average)

A. Earth's axis of 24-hour rotation tilts at an angle of 23□°

B. The elliptical orbit of Earth around the Sun changes the distance of the Sun from Earth

C. The southern hemisphere has more water than the northern hemisphere

D. The green house effect is greater for the northern hemisphere

Answer: B. The elliptical orbit of Earth around the Sun changes the distance of the Sun from Earth
The tilt of Earth's axis causes the seasons. The Earth is close to the Sun during winter in the northern hemisphere. Winter in the southern hemisphere occurs six months later when Earth is farther from the Sun. The presence of water explains why winters are harsher inland than by the coast.

9. **Which of the following facts of physics best explains the cause of tides? *(Rigorous)***

A. The density of water is less than the density of rock

B. The force of gravity follows the inverse square law

C. Centripetal acceleration causes water on Earth to bulge

D. The gravitational force of the Moon on Earth's oceans

Answer: B. The force of gravity follows the inverse square law
The main cause of lunar tides is that the Moon's gravitational force is greater on water near the Moon than on the other side of Earth. This causes the bulge of water. Earth's rotation causes the location of the bulge to change. Centripetal acceleration causes Earth's water to bulge and affects tides caused by the Sun's gravity, however, the effect is minor.

10. **Which of the following is not a property that eukaryotes have and prokaryotes do not have? *(Average)***

A. Nucleus

B. Ribosomes

C. Chromosomes

D. Mitochondria

Answer: B. Ribosomes
Prokaryotes do not have a nuclear membrane, and the DNA is not packed into chromosomes. Mitochondria are organelles that produce power are not in the smaller, simpler cell. Ribosomes are the sites where cells assemble proteins.

11. **Which of the following processes and packages macromolecules?**
(Easy)

A. Lysosomes

B. Cytosol

C. Golgi apparatus

D. Plastids

Answer: C. Golgi apparatus
Lysosomes contain digestive enzymes. Cytosol is the liquid inside cells. Plastids manufacture chemicals used in plant cells.

12. **Which is not a characteristic of living organisms?**
(Easy)

A. Sexual reproduction

B. Ingestion

C. Synthesis

D. Respiration

Answer: A. Sexual reproduction
Only certain organisms reproduce sexually, that is by mixing DNA. Single-celled organisms generally reproduce by cell division. Ingestion means taking nutrients from outside the cell wall. Synthesis means creating new cellular material. Respiration means generating energy by combining oxygen or some other gas with material in the cell.

13. At what stage in mitosis does the chromatin become chromosomes? *(Average)*

A. Telophase

B. Anaphase

C. Prophase

D. Metaphase

Answer: C. Prophase
Prophase is the beginning of mitosis. In metaphase, fibers attach to chromosomes, and in anaphase, the chromosomes separate. In telophase, the cells divide.

14. Meiosis starts with a single cell and ends with which of the following? *(Average)*

A. Two diploid cells

B. Two haploid cells

C. Four diploid cells

D. Four haploid cells

Answer: D. Four haploid cells
The single cell that begins the creation of a gamete has a full set of chromosomes in matched pairs. This is called a diploid cell. After the first division there are two haploid cells. After the second division, there are four haploid cells.

15. How many autosomes are in a somatic cells of human beings? *(Easy)*

A. 22

B. 23

C. 44

D. 46

Answer: C. 44
The total number of chromosomes is 46, but two of them are the sex chromosomes. Autosomes refer to the chromosomes that are not X or Y chromosomes.

16. Which of the following is not part of Darwinian evolution? *(Average)*

A. Survival of the fittest

B. Random mutations

C. Heritability of acquired traits

D. Natural selection

Answer: C. Heritability of acquired traits
Acquired traits change somatic cells but not gametes. So they are not passed on to succeeding generations. Natural selection occurs because offspring through random mutations are more fit than others to survive. The idea that acquired traits can be passed on to offspring is called Lamarkism.

17. Taxonomy classifies species into genera (plural of genus) based on similarities. Species are subordinate to genera. The most general or highest taxonomical group is the kingdom. Which of the following is the correct order of the other groups from highest to lowest?
(Easy)

A. Class $\Rightarrow$ order$\Rightarrow$ family $\Rightarrow$ phylum

B. Phylum $\Rightarrow$ class $\Rightarrow$ family $\Rightarrow$ order

C. Phylum $\Rightarrow$ class $\Rightarrow$ order $\Rightarrow$ family

D. Order $\Rightarrow$ phylum $\Rightarrow$ class $\Rightarrow$ family

Answer: C. Phylum $\Rightarrow$ class $\Rightarrow$ order $\Rightarrow$ family
In the case of the domestic dog, the genus (Canis) includes wolves, the family (Canidae) includes jackals and coyotes, the order (Carnivore) includes lions, the class (Mammals) includes mice, and the phylum (Chordata) includes fish.

18. Which of the following describes the interaction between community members when one species feeds of another species but does not kill it immediately?
(Easy)

A. Parasitism

B. Predation

C. Commensalism

D. Mutualism

Answer: A. Parasitism
Predation occurs when one species kills another species. In mutualism, both species benefit. In commensalisms, one species benefits without the other being harmed.

19. Which of the following statements about the density of a substance is true?
(Easy)

A. It is a chemical property

B. It is a physical property

C. It does not depend on the temperature of the substance

D. It is a property only of liquids and solids

Answer: B. It is a physical property
The density of a substance is the mass of an object made of the substance divided by the object's volume. Chemical properties involve chemical reactions. Densities of substances generally decrease with higher temperatures.

20. The electrons in a neutral atom that is not in an excited energy state are in various energy shells. For example, there are two electrons in the lowest energy shell and eight in the next shell if the atom contains more than 10 electrons. How many electrons are in the shell with the maximum number of electrons?
(Easy)

A. 8

B. 18

C. 32

D. 44

Answer: C. 32
There is no energy level with 44 electrons. There is however, a shell with 18 electrons. The number of electrons in an atom's outer shell determines how the atom chemically interacts with other atoms.

21. Which statement best explains why a balance scale is used to measure both weight and mass?
(Rigorous)

A. The weight and mass of an object are identical concepts

B. The force of gravity between two objects depends on the mass of the two objects

C. Inertial mass and gravitational mass are identical

D. A balance scale compares the weight of two objects

Answer: C. Inertial mass and gravitational mass are identical
The mass of an object is a fundamental property of matter and is measured in kilograms. The weight is the force of gravity between Earth and an object near Earth's surface and is measured in newtons or pounds. Newton's second law ($F = ma$) and the universal law of gravity ($F = G\frac{m_{\text{earth}}m}{d^2}$) determine the weight of an object. The mass in Newton's second law is called the inertial mass and the mass in the universal law of gravity is called the gravitational mass. The two kinds of masses are identical.

22. Which of the following does not determine the frictional force between a box sliding down a ramp?
(Average)

A. The weight of the box

B. The area of the box

C. The angle the ramp makes with the horizontal

D. The chemical properties of the two surfaces

Answer: B. The area of the box
The frictional force is caused by bonding between the molecules of the box with the molecules of the ramp. At a small number of points, there is contact between the molecules. While there may be a small increase in the frictional force as the area increases, it is not noticeable. The main determinant of the frictional force is the weight of the box and the nature of the two surfaces.

23. **Which statement is true about temperature?**
(Easy)

A. Temperature is a measurement of heat

B. Temperature is how hot or cold an object is

C. The coldest temperature ever measured is zero degrees Kelvin

D. The temperature of a molecule is its kinetic energy

Answer: B. Temperature is how hot or cold an object is
Temperature is a physical property of objects relating to how they feel when touched. For example, 0 degrees Celsius or 32 degrees Fahrenheit is defined as the temperature of ice water. Heat is a form of energy that flows from hot objects in thermal contact with cold objects. The greater the temperature of an object, the greater the kinetic energy of the molecules making up the object, but a single molecule does not have a temperature. The third law of thermodynamics is that absolute zero can never be achieved in a laboratory.

24. **When glass is heated, it becomes softer and softer until it becomes a liquid. Which of the following statements best describes this phenomenon?**
(Rigorous)

A. Glass has no heat of vaporization

B. Glass has no heat of fusion

C. The latent heat of glass is zero calories per gram

D. Glass is made up of crystals

Answer: B. Glass has no heat of fusion
When a substance goes from the solid state to the liquid state as heat is added at the melting point, the temperature is constant. All the heat energy goes into changing the forces between the atoms, ions, or molecules so that the substance becomes a liquid. The heat of vaporization is the calories of heat needed to change one gram of the liquid into a gas.

25. Which statement could be described as the first law of thermodynamics?
(Average)

A. No machine can convert heat energy to work with 100 percent efficiency

B. Energy is neither created nor destroyed

C. Thermometers can be used to measure temperatures

D. Heat flows from hot objects to cold objects

Answer: B. Energy is neither created nor destroyed
The first law of thermodynamics is considered to be a statement of the conservation of energy. Choices B and D are statements of the second law of thermodynamics. Answer C is the zeroth law of thermodynamics.

26. What kind of chemical reaction is the burning of coal?
(Average)

A. Exothermic and composition

B. Exothermic and decomposition

C. Endothermic and composition

D. Exothermic and decomposition

Answer: A. Exothermic and composition
Burning coal means oxygen is combining with carbon to produce carbon dioxide. Since heat is released, the reaction is exothermic. Since elements are combining to for a compound, the reaction is a composition.

27. **Which of the following is a result of a nuclear reaction called fission?**
(Easy)

A. Sunlight

B. Cosmic radiation

C. Supernova

D. Existence of the elements in the periodic table

Answer: D. Existence of the elements in the periodic table
Sunlight comes from fusion. Cosmic radiation has many sources. Inside stars, hydrogen and helium combine to form the higher elements on the periodic table.

28. **What is technology?**
(Easy)

A. The application of science to satisfy human needs

B. Knowledge of complex machines, computer systems, and manufacturing processes

C. The study of engineering

D. A branch of science

Answer: A. The application of science to satisfy human needs
Science is knowledge of the universe gained by observations and experiments. Technology is the use of this knowledge to help human beings.

29. An experiment is performed to determine how the surface area of a liquid affects how long it takes for the liquid to evaporate. One hundred milliliters of water is put in containers with surface areas of 10 cm^2, 30 cm^2, 50 cm^2, 70 cm^2, and 90 cm^2. The time it took for each container to evaporate is recorded. Which of the following is a controlled variable?
(Average)

A. The time required for each evaporation

B. The area of the surfaces

C. The amount of water

D. The temperature of the water

Answer: C. The amount of water
The surface area is the independent variable and the time is the dependent variable. The temperature of the water should have been controlled in this experiment.

30. Stars near Earth can be seen to move relative to fixed stars. In observing the motion of a nearby star over a period of decades, an astronomer notices that the path is not a straight line but wobbles about a straight line. The astronomer reports in a peer-reviewed journal that a planet is rotating around the star, causing it to wobble. Which of the following statements best describes the proposition that the star has a planet?
(Rigorous)

A. Observation

B. Hypothesis

C. Theory

D. Inference

Answer: D. Inference
The observation in the report was the wobbly path of the star. It would be a hypothesis if this was the basis of a further experiment or observation about the existence of the planet. A theory would be more speculative. The astronomer didn't just suggest that the planet was there; the report stated that the star has a planet.

Answer Key: Science

1. A
2. A
3. B
4. C
5. D
6. B
7. B
8. B
9. B
10. B
11. C
12. A
13. C
14. D
15. C
16. C
17. C
18. A
19. B
20. C
21. C
22. B
23. B
24. B
25. B
26. A
27. D
28. A
29. C
30. D

Rigor Table: Science

	Easy 56.7%	**Average 30%**	**Rigorous 13.3%**
Questions	**1, 2, 3, 4, 5, 6 ,7, 11, 12, 15, 17, 18, 19, 20, 23, 27, 28**	**8, 10, 13, 14, 16, 22, 25, 26, 29**	**9, 21, 24, 30**

CPSIA information can be obtained at www.ICGtesting.com
Printed in the USA
BVOW05s1537201015

423326BV00005B/45/P

9 781607 872610